PADDLING ARIZONA

A Guide to Lakes, Rivers, and Creeks

by Tyler Williams

Funhog Press
Flagstaff, Arizona

Flatwater Rivers and Lakes

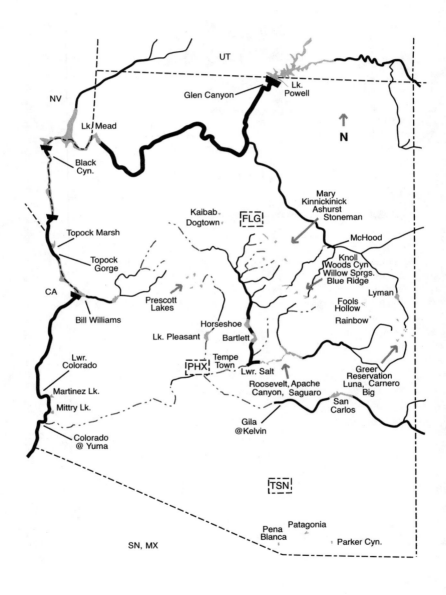

Alphabetical Listing of Flatwater Rivers and Lakes

Apache Lake	pg.56	Lyman Lake	pg.108
Ashurst Lake	pg.86	Lynx Lake	pg.100
Bartlett Lake	pg.52	Martinez Lake	pg.70
Big Lake	pg.114	Mary (Lake)	pg.84
Bill Williams River Mouth	pg.68	McHood Park Lake	pg.46
Black Canyon	pg.8	Mead (Lake)	pg.42
Blue Ridge Reservoir	pg.92	Parker Canyon Lake	pg.120
Bunch Reservoir	pg.112	Patagonia Lake	pg.74
Canyon Lake	pg.58	Pena Blanca Lake	pg.76
Carnero Lake	pg.110	Pleasant (Lake)	pg.48
Colorado River (lower)	pg.12	Powell (Lake)	pg.38
Colorado @ Yuma	pg.16	Prescott Granite Lakes	pg.102
Dogtown Reservoir	pg.82	Prescott Pine Lakes	pg.100
Fools Hollow Lake	pg.104	Rainbow Lake	pg.106
Gila River @ Kelvin	pg.32	Reservation Lake	pg.118
Goldwater Lake	pg.100	River Reservoir	pg.112
Glen Canyon	pg.20	Roosevelt Lake	pg.54
Greer Lakes	pg.112	Saguaro Lake	pg.60
Horseshoe Reservoir	pg.50	Salt River (Lower)	pg.28
Kaibab Lake	pg.80	San Carlos Reservoir	pg.64
Kinnickinnick Lake	pg.88	Stoneman Lake	pg.90
Knoll Lake	pg.94	Topock Gorge	pg.24
Lake Mary	pg.84	Topock Marsh	pg.66
Lake Mead	pg.42	Tempe Town Lake	pg.62
Lake Pleasant	pg.48	Tunnel Reservoir	pg.112
Lake Powell	pg.38	Watson Lake	pg.102
Lower Colorado River	pg.12	Willow Springs Lake	pg.98
Lower Salt River	pg.28	Willow Lake	pg.102
Luna Lake	pg.116	Woods Canyon Lake	pg.96

Disclaimer

Paddling is dangerous. Other dangerous activities commonly practiced while on paddling trips include, but are not limited to: portaging, swimming, drinking the water, and driving to and from your destination. Nearly everything about a paddling trip is dangerous. If you don't want to endanger your life, don't go paddling, don't buy this book, and certainly don't use this book.

Nature is constantly changing. Rockslides occur, floods change river and creek channels, beaches erode away, and earthquakes create new terrain altogether. Therefore, any information contained herein should be considered out of date and possibly incorrect.

The author and publisher of *Paddling Arizona* claims no responsibility for any actions that might be embarked upon through the use of this book. Any decision that you, the reader, makes to climb, swim, walk, sit, stand, sleep, eat, or drink is entirely your own. As a living creature on this planet, you are burdened with the responsibility to take care of yourself. Any trouble you get into, before or after reading this book, is entirely your problem, and nobody else's. No amount of guidance, either from a guidebook or otherwise, can replace personal judgment.

Copyright © 2009 by Tyler Williams

Published by Funhog Press
www.funhogpress.com

All rights reserved. No part of this book may be reproduced in any way. This includes, but is not limited to, unauthorized posting on the world wide web or internet. Written permission from the author is needed for any use other than brief quotations in reviews.

ISBN 0-9664919-4-4

Edited by Ginny Gelczis, Lisa Gelczis, Roy Lippman
Designed by Mary Williams, www.marywilliamsdesign.com
Cover photos by Tyler Williams
Photos by Tyler Williams, Lisa Gelczis, Eli Butler

Table of Contents

OVERVIEW MAP — ii

ALPHABETICAL LISTING OF CANYONS — iii

INTRODUCTION — 0

ACKNOWLEDGEMENTS — 1

ARIZONA BOATING SEASONS — 2

HOW TO USE THIS BOOK — 3

RESPECT — 5

FLATWATER RIVERS — 7
- Black Canyon — 8
- Lower Colorado River — 12
- Colorado River @ Yuma — 16
- Glen Canyon — 20
- Topock Gorge — 24
- Lower Salt River — 28
- Gila River (Kelvin run) — 32

DESERT LAKES — 37
- Lake Powell — 38
- Lake Mead — 42
- McHood Park Lake — 46
- Lake Pleasant — 48
- Horseshoe Reservoir — 50
- Bartlett Lake — 52
- Roosevelt Lake — 54
- Apache Lake — 56
- Canyon Lake — 58
- Saguaro Lake — 60
- Tempe Town Lake — 62
- San Carlos Reservoir — 64
- Topock Marsh — 66
- Bill Williams River Mouth — 68
- Martinez Lake — 70
- Mittry Lake — 72
- Patagonia Lake — 74
- Pena Blanca Lake — 76

HIGH COUNTRY LAKES	79
Kaibab Lake	80
Dogtown Reservoir	82
Lake Mary	84
Ashurst Lake	86
Kinnickinnick Lake	88
Stoneman Lake	90
Blue Ridge Reservoir	92
Knoll Lake	94
Woods Canyon Lake	96
Willow Springs Lake	98
Prescott Pine-Tree Lakes (Goldwater, Lynx)	100
Prescott Granite Lakes (Willow, Watson)	102
Fools Hollow Lake	104
Rainbow Lake	106
Lyman Lake	108
Carnero Lake	110
Greer Lakes (Bunch, River, Tunnel)	112
Big Lake	114
Luna Lake	116
Reservation Lake	118
Parker Canyon Lake	120
WHITEWATER RIVERS INTRODUCTION	123
Little Colorado River (LCR Gorge)	136
Chinle Creek	140
Paria River	141
Oak Creek (Indian Gardens run)	142
Little Colorado (Grand Falls run)	146
Oak Creek (upper reaches)	146
Oak Creek (Sedona - Red Rock Crossing)	148
Pumphouse Wash	152
Munds Canyon	153
Beaver Creek	156
Oak Creek (lower reaches)	158
Dry Creek	159
Verde River (White Bridge - Beasley)	160
Woods Canyon	162
Rattlesnake Canyon	163
Verde River (Beasley - Gap Creek or Childs)	164
Upper Verde (Perkinsville - TAPCO)	168
Wet Beaver Creek	168
Hell Canyon	169
Verde River (Childs - Horseshoe Reservoir)	170

West Clear Creek (wilderness run)	174
Lower West Clear Creek	175
Fossil Creek	176
Lower Verde (Horseshoe - Salt River)	180
Agua Fria River	182
Black Canyon	186
Poland Creek	186
Sycamore Creek (Butterfly Canyon)	187
Turkey Creek	187
East Verde (day stretch)	188
Lower East Verde (wilderness run)	190
East Verde (park & huck)	192
Christopher Creek	194
Tonto Creek (Hellsgate)	198
Tonto Creek (Lower Gorge)	202
Tonto Creek (Headwaters)	206
Salome Creek	207
Salt River (daily)	208
Salt River (wilderness)	212
Upper Black River	216
Upper Little Colorado	218
East Clear Creek	222
Chevelon Creek	223
San Francisco River	224
Blue River	226
Gila Box	228
Eagle Creek	230
Burro Creek	232
Virgin River (Freeway Gorge)	236
Santa Maria River (Highway 93 run)	238
Santa Maria River (lower reaches)	240
Santa Maria River (upper box)	242
Bill Williams River	245
Grand Canyon	246

Introduction

"Paddling in *Arizona?*" I have heard this skeptical response innumerable times during the creation of this book. I must admit that I, too, have tempered my enthusiasm for this project when given the dubious prospects of selling a paddling guide for a desert region. This is partly why it has taken several years for this book to go from concept to fruition.

Originally, *Paddling Arizona* was proposed as purely a whitewater guide, an idea which my wife, Lisa, claims to have proposed. The origins of this project remains a matter of domestic banter in our household, but in any case "that Arizona paddling book" as we've vaguely referred to it has been a handy excuse for both of us to go boating for many years now.

Alas, we both realized that the book tentatively titled *Arizona Rivers— Brown Water, White Knuckles* would be a true labor of love with little sales potential. The book's scope was thus expanded to cover Southwestern rivers including New Mexico, Utah, and portions of Colorado. Thorough research for this large area proved daunting, however, and good guides already existed for those locales outside of Arizona. Prudently, the book went to the back burner.

The idea of including lakes and flatwater routes in the guide emerged slowly. I bought a touring boat. I began to explore flatwater locales. I saw huge potential. I began to write things down.

Recreational lake paddling and touring opened a whole new world for me that was ripe with beauty and adventure. As I traveled across the state exploring new reservoirs and rivers, the possibilities of flatwater boating expanded. I found myself enjoying many of the same experiences that first drew me to river running: camping at water's edge, watching wildlife from the quiet of my boat, feeling the glide of water beneath me. Yes, flatwater paddling, it turned out, was pretty cool.

In addition to introducing me to a new realm of outdoor adventure, flatwater seemed the perfect avenue to introduce more people to the peace and beauty and majesty of the outdoors. "That Arizona paddling book" we had talked about came back to the fore. It would encompass all paddling, from the quietest lake to the steepest creek.

As with all my guidebooks, I hope this one facilitates a greater awareness and appreciation of the natural world by introducing readers to places that have borne inspiration in me.

The fact that this book's destinations all center on water makes our connection to nature even more poignant. The Southwest is an arid place where water is especially precious. By visiting our waterways, seeing where our water comes from, and understanding how it is managed, we can be better informed in our decisions regarding water use, be it at the kitchen sink or the ballot box. Per usual, I am probably preaching to the choir here, because if you picked up this book you likely have a greater awareness of

Introduction 1

water issues than the average American. Still, I hope *Paddling Arizona* will make some difference by building a constituency of water-valuing people. If one less driveway is wastefully washed with a water hose, or one less sprinkler is left running in the rain, I'll feel less guilt with the publication of *Paddling Arizona*.

Yes, guilt. It's not a healthy emotion, but one that is inherent in the work of a guidebook writer, at least this guidebook writer. Prior to the publication of this book, many waterways of Arizona were virtually unknown. For me and the few locals who made the effort to seek out these hidden locales, Arizona was our secret stash. Now the secret is out. Although I doubt Arizona is ever going to become a paddling Mecca, traffic at put-ins and launch ramps will no doubt increase with this guide. Those of us who are discouraged at the exposure of our backyard playgrounds might find solace in this: There's still more out there.

It has taken years of research to complete *Paddling Arizona*, and I still haven't paddled everything on my list. Finally, though, I had to say "enough!" This title's time had finally come. I hope you can share in the fruits of my fun.

Acknowledgements

My name might be on the title of this book, but there are many others who have contributed.

My mother must be given credit for instilling me with the energy and interest in exploring the outdoors. At age 83, she is still game for new adventures. My father shared his wisdom, and passed on some of his unfaltering confidence. Without either of these tools, it is doubtful that I would finish any book project. Thank you, Lisa: my paddling partner, business consultant, photo model, photographer, editor, science adviser, friend, girlfriend, wife, and much more. Life would be waaay different without you.

I am very appreciative of my editing team: Ginny Gelczis, and Roy Lippman. Thanks to Jeri Ledbetter for flying me around so I could take aerial photos. Thank you Donita Polly at the USGS library for your map and research help. Thanks to Bill Burger, Mike Lopez, Scott Reager, and Jim Warnicke of AZ Game & Fish for answering my lake questions. Thanks to Annette Smits at the Tonto National Forest, and Diana Fister with the city of Prescott for updating lake information. Thanks to Robert Finlay, who helped out with tips on Lake Mead paddling. Thanks to Debbie and Grant at Yuma city hall for helping me out when I did my research on the Lower Colorado. Thanks to Pete Zwagerman for info on Phoenix area rivers.

Last but not least, thanks to all my boating partners who have loaned me gear, bought the beer, driven the shuttle, paddled into my pictures, held the rope, saved my life, shared their stories, rallied to load boats at 6 a.m., and just been there to hang out with. You're all a part of this book.

Arizona Boating Seasons

For flatwater paddling, Arizona offers year-round opportunities. With the wide range of climates and environments found in the state, paddling excursions can be enjoyed any day of the year.

Summertime is the season to enjoy the high country lakes. Few settings are as peaceful as a glassy pond in the White Mountains on a cool August morning. As the day begins to warm, soft white thunderheads billow. By afternoon, it is time to scamper for shelter as those same beautiful clouds unleash furious storms.

Low elevation desert waterways are certainly paddleable in the summer months, too. In fact, they are some of the few habitable places that exist in our summertime deserts. There are disadvantages to paddling the desert in summer, however. If you thought the thunderstorms of the mountains were fierce, you should see the speedboat crowds on a desert lake during a July weekend.

Autumn is a better time to explore desert waters. The crowds have thinned somewhat, and warm afternoon temperatures make life on the water pleasant. Migratory bird species begin to show up, and skies are often a cobalt blue. Mountain lakes are also excellent destinations throughout the fall. Evenings are brisk, however, and early snowfalls can force the closure of access roads.

Winter turns mountain paddling locales into wilderness skating rinks, but most locations below 5,000 feet remain ice-free. This is the time to find quiet on Arizona's desert waters. Afternoon temperatures are often in the 60s, with bright sunshine. Winter storms can bring periods of cold rain to the desert, but these rainy days also clean the atmosphere of pollutants, bringing post-storm crystalline freshness—glorious paddling weather.

Springtime bursts with desert wildflowers and warmer temperatures, prompting many of us to head for the outdoors. Beware of horrendously gusty winds during this time, however. As the spring storm track speeds by the state to the north, and the sun rapidly heats the Southwestern deserts, Arizona's windy season arrives. Open waters can become a nasty chop, turning a mellow afternoon paddle into an unwanted high-seas adventure. By the time the spring winds arrive, snow is melting in the high country and the forests are becoming green again, making way for another summer morning on a glassy mountain lake.

How to use this book

Flatwater River Descriptions
General Description: A general statement about the river's characteristics.
Motorized Traffic: A rating of Low, Moderate, or High will be used. *Low* indicates minimal motor usage. You might see a motorboat on these river stretches, but it is not the norm. A *Moderate* rating is given to waterways that usually have some motor use, but are not speedways of gas fumes and noise. *High* motorized traffic means motorboats dominate the scene. Paddlers will have to make special plans to avoid motorboats on these rivers. This can be accomplished, however. Even on rivers with heavy motor use, off-season and midweek excursions often produce quiet waters with limited motorboats.
Difficulty: A rating of Easy, Moderate, or Advanced will be provided. *Easy* means that there are few complex currents, and a first-time paddler should be able to make the run. *Moderate* indicates that there are some hazards on the river. A first-time paddler will still probably be okay here if they are accompanied by a more experienced paddler. *Advanced* flatwater rivers are one step below whitewater. Expect fast current and noticeable eddylines. The lower Salt and the Gila below Kelvin could be considered whitewater rivers. Both are small and fast waterways compared with the other flatwater rivers in this book. They are listed among the flatwater rivers, however, because their appeal is more congruent with a flatwater paddler's expectations. Both these rivers should be considered transition runs between flatwater and whitewater paddling.
Length: The distance in miles of the described run.
Gage: The title of the USGS gage on the internet (Here's the website: http://waterdata.usgs.gov/az/nwis/current/?type=flow) that indicates river flow for the particular river stretch.
Shuttle: The shuttle distance required for the described run. Also listed are road surfaces, and whether the shuttle is a good candidate for hitchhiking or bicycling.
Best Season: The months that I consider the best time to paddle the particular stretch.

Lake Descriptions
*There are almost no natural lakes in Arizona, just a few swampy low spots that fill during times of high water. The terms "lake" and "reservoir" are used interchangeably in this book.
General Description: A brief overview of the lake's characteristics.
Motorized Traffic: A rating of Low, Moderate, or High will be used. *Low* indicates minimal motor usage. Many lakes have motor restrictions of 8 or 10 horsepower maximums, or single electric motors only, or no

motors at all. These lakes would all qualify for a Low rating. Even if a lake has no restrictions, but the motor use is generally light, a Low rating will be given. A *Moderate* rating is given to waterways that usually have some motor use, but are not speedways of gas fumes and noise. *High* motorized traffic means motorboats dominate the scene. Paddlers will have to make special plans to avoid motorboats on these reservoirs. This can be accomplished, however. Even on heavy motor use lakes, off-season and midweek excursions often provide for open waters with fewer motorboats.

Surface area when full: The surface area of the lake in acres. In most cases, these figures were taken from a governmental geographic database based on full pool levels. Many Arizona lakes are often less than full pool.

Shoreline when full: The shoreline of a given lake, in miles, when it is at full pool.

Fish Species: The fish species that inhabit the lake as reported by the Arizona Department of Game and Fish or other managing agency. Not every fish species that has inhabited the lake is always listed. The species listed are the ones most commonly found. Fishing licenses are required on all the lakes in this book, either from the AZ Game and Fish Department or a specific tribe if you are on reservation lands.

Elevation: The elevation of the lake, in feet, above sea level as it exists in the year 2006. Sea level on our warming planet is currently rising.

Best Season: What I consider to be the optimal season for visiting a certain lake. Many mountain lakes are frozen or inaccessible in winter. Desert lakes can be paddled anytime, but winter is generally more pleasant and less crowded. For more information on paddling seasons, see "Arizona Boating Seasons" in the introduction.

Acronyms

cfs: Cubic Feet per Second. This is the standard unit of measure for streamflows in the United States.

fpm: Feet Per Mile. This is the standard unit of measure for stream gradient in the United States.

mp: Milepost—a unit of measure on most roads and highways.

R-E-S-P-E-C-T

As outdoor recreation has grown within our culture, the question of how to treat the natural environment has spawned numerous catch phrases, rules, and reminders that are almost omnipresent: "Pack it in, pack it out," "Leave no trace." Sadly, these admonishments are not enough to make an impression with a certain percentage of people, and most of our natural areas see negative impacts from human visitation. As paddlers, we should try to mitigate these impacts as much as possible. Below are a few tips that we might find helpful in harmonizing with the natural world. Really, though, low-impact camping, hiking, paddling, or whatever can be summed up by one word: **RESPECT!**

If we pay attention and respect the world around us—fellow paddlers, other lake users, other mammals, birds, fish, insects, trees, grasses, rocks—we will not have to remember the infinite rules that really just remind us of the same thing—show respect!

Beyond that, here are a few tips on special situations that might arise while paddling in Arizona.

1) Watch wildlife carefully and quietly. Are they aware of you? And if so, are you freaking them out? Respect their space. The most rewarding wildlife watching occurs when animals are acting naturally.

2) Be careful with your micro-trash. It's doubtful anyone reading this book will leave their 30-pack of beer cans smoldering in the fire pit, but we might lose track of the small stuff. Do a visual sweep of your camp when leaving, and keep your eyes peeled for little bits of foil and unnatural materials that will virtually never decompose.

3) Don't spread invasives. Non-native algaes and invertebrates can severely alter river and lake ecosystems. Stop the spread of these environmental havoc-wreakers by cleaning off your gear (boat, paddle, wet clothes) before leaving one lake or river and entering another.

4) Crap carefully. Go a few hundred yards away from the water and get well off the trail in a random spot to take a dump. Bury your feces. Don't ever leave toilet paper behind. Burn it (without starting a forest fire), pack it out (a small ziploc bag works fine), or don't use any in the first place. Wiping your butt with a stick or rock once in a while won't kill you. In heavily used areas without toilet facilities, it is best to pack out your waste. River runners are well aware of this practice, as it is a requirement on many popular rivers. A military surplus ammo can is still the toilet of choice for packing out your waste. Various septic and waste treatment facilities can clean these portable toilets.

5) Take a camp that suits your size. It is common etiquette for small groups to take smaller camps, and leave larger camps for larger groups. It is preferable to keep your group small when possible. Big crowds increase impacts on the land exponentially.

FLATWATER RIVERS

Black Canyon

General Description: A popular river/lake stretch in a spectacular setting
Motorized Traffic: Moderate (Black Canyon is closed to motors on Sundays and Mondays)
Difficulty: Easy
Length: 12 miles
Gage: Lake Mohave at Davis Dam (The lower the lake, the more current you'll have.)
Shuttle: 15 miles, licensed concessionaire required to put-in below Boulder Dam. Call Desert River Kayak 888-529-2533, or Desert Adventures 702-293-5026 or Jerkwater 928-768-7753. Regardless of who provides your shuttle, you must contact Black Canyon River Adventures 702-294-1414 to arrange reservations and permits for launching.
Best Season: November — March
Peak Flow: pre-dam—300,000 cfs July 1884

The first thing you should know about paddling Black Canyon is that it is not a wilderness experience. Jumbo jets and tourist-toting helicopters create a constant din of air traffic overhead, motorboats cruise the river, and throngs of hikers flock to the nearby hot springs.

That said, Black Canyon is a spectacular place. Steep and narrow side canyons hold running streams of geothermally heated water, springs drip from fern covered walls, and striking cliffs of volcanic rock plunge into deep clear river water.

Although there is current most of the way from the dam to the take-out at Willow Beach, the river only seems like a real river for the first couple miles below the dam. Below here, it is a lake with a tiny bit of residual current coursing through.

There is an interesting sauna cave just below the put-in on the right, where a tunnel built during dam construction tapped a geothermal vein. Other hot springs are located just downstream at Goldstrike Canyon, and at Boy Scout Canyon, located a mile below Goldstrike on the right. Boy Scout Canyon also provides a dramatic aided canyoneering route, often with ropes leading up tepid waterfalls in a narrow gorge.

The best soaking pools on the trip are found at the Arizona Hot Springs on river left, adjacent to the once formidable Ringbolt Rapid. There is a popular trail leading to these springs from the highway, so privacy is rarely a possibility. Nonetheless, the hot pools pinched in canyon narrows are a natural wonder not to be missed. Keep your head out of the water when soaking, because you'll be sharing the water with the potentially deadly Naegleria fowleri. This amoeba can enter your nose and cause a lethal

Pulling into camp in Black Canyon

brain infection.

On that note, remember that Black Canyon has its drawbacks, but it is still an Arizona paddling experience that I highly recommend.

Logistics: Permits are required to launch at the base of Portal Road below Boulder (a.k.a. Hoover) Dam. Currently, the Bureau of Reclamation and National Park Service are contracted with Black Canyon/Willow Beach River Adventures 702-293-8204, who handles reservations and permits for Black Canyon. There is currently a $13 fee per person to launch, and you must show identification prior to launching.

Rugged volcanic surroundings near Willow Beach

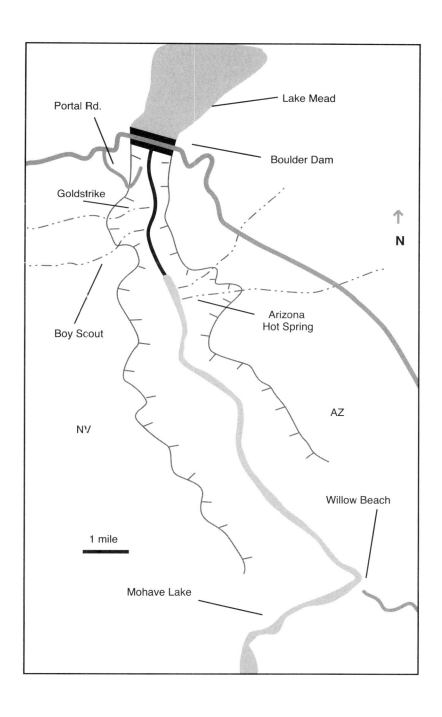

Lower Colorado River

General Description: A relatively undeveloped segment of the Colorado River in the Mojave Desert
Motorized Traffic: Moderate
Difficulty: Easy
Length: 22 miles from Walters Camp to Picacho Recreation Area / 33 miles from Walters Camp to Martinez Lake or Fishers Landing / 40 miles from Walters Camp to Squaw Lake
Gage: Colorado River below Palo Verde Dam
Shuttle: Walters Camp to Picacho: 86 miles / Walters Camp to Ferguson Lake: 87 miles / Walters Camp to Martinez Lake, Fishers Landing: 100 miles / Walters Camp to Squaw Lake: 80 miles
Best Season: November — February
Peak Flow: pre-dam—300,000 cfs July 1884, post-dam—42,400 cfs, February 8, 1937

About 30 miles downstream from Blythe, the Colorado River corridor starts to change from inhabited farmland to mostly uninhabited desert. The river maintains a good 2 to 4 mph current, but there are no rapids, and only a few small eddylines. Speedboats and personal watercraft do travel the river, but in winter their numbers are small and scattered. It is possible, or even likely, to go for days without seeing a motorboat. This relatively wild character continues for 40 miles along the lower Colorado, until Imperial Dam signals a transition back to more agricultural environs. Most of the undeveloped 40 mile stretch lies within two wildlife refuges, the Cibola and the Imperial.

Camping is not permitted in either refuge, but overnight trips are possible by camping at Picacho State Recreation Area, or Ferguson Lake, both on the California side of the river. Camping at Picacho is restricted to developed sites which are outfitted with portable toilets, garbage cans, and picnic tables. The sites are available on a first come first serve basis for $1.50 a night per person. Besides being the only legal camping locations, these camps are really the only potential campsites that exist through here, as the river banks are lined with impenetrable thickets of river cane and cattail.

Getting through the riparian jungle is next to impossible in most places, but an intriguing desert of jagged volcanic mountains awaits beyond the river corridor. This is one of the hottest and driest deserts in the world. Floating through this landscape on a cool clear river offers one of the most splendid juxtapositions available in adventure travel.

There are a few different trip options for paddling the lower Colorado, and all of them involve lengthy shuttles. As a long day trip, or an

Flatwater Rivers 13

Down the lazy river...

overnight, Walters Camp to Picacho Recreation Area is a good choice.

After leaving Walters Camp, the river flows through remote Paradise Valley before reaching the boundary of Picacho Recreation Area a dozen miles downstream. It is then another 8 miles to the main boat ramp at Picacho. Backwater lakes in the river's floodplain offer some of the best bird watching and interesting swamp paddling along the lower Colorado, and two of these, Taylor Lake and Adobe Lake, are easily accessed in the miles above the Picacho ramp.

Below Picacho, the river takes a west to east course as it cuts through the Trigo Mountains, then swings south upon reaching the flatlands on the far side. Ferguson Lake, about 10 miles below Picacho on river right, offers camping and take-out possibilities. Martinez Lake and Fishers Landing, both a couple miles past Ferguson on river left, are other take-out options. It can be difficult to spot the channel openings that lead to certain access points, so scout your take-out ahead of time.

For the most paddling with the shortest shuttle, continue all the way to Squaw Lake on the California side. This will provide just over 40 miles of paddling with about 80 miles of shuttling.

Logistics: All of the take-out points (Ferguson Lake, Martinez Lake, Fishers Landing, Squaw Lake) except Picacho Recreation Area are most easily reached by taking Highway 95 north out of Yuma. It is about 17 miles from Yuma to Imperial Dam Rd., which leads across the river to the California side. A few miles after entering California, there is a signed turn for both Squaw Lake and Ferguson Lake. The road into Squaw Lake is paved, the road to Ferguson is gravel. The turn for Martinez Lake and Fishers Landing is about 20 miles north of Yuma on Highway 95, located between mileposts 46 and 47. It is about 10.5 miles along this undulating desert highway past America's WMDs to both take-outs.

To reach Picacho Recreation Area, take the Winterhaven/4th Ave. exit off I-8 westbound, veer right off the exit ramp, and take the first right turn. It is 22 miles on Picacho Road to the riverside camp area. Most of this distance is on washboard gravel roads.

To reach Walters Camp, take I-8 west out of Yuma about 10 miles to the Ogilby Road exit. Head north on Ogilby Road over 20 miles to Highway 78, and continue north about 17 miles to Walters Camp Road. It is about 7 miles down Walters Camp Road to the old river channel where the launch area is. Paddle south from the launch ramp to reach the main river.

Flatwater Rivers 15

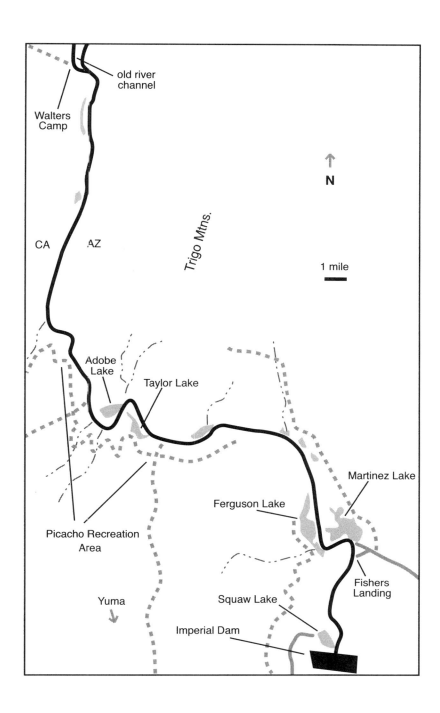

Colorado River @ Yuma
(Yuma Daily)

General Description: A river float leading through downtown Yuma
Motorized Traffic: Low
Difficulty: Moderate
Length: 5 miles
Gage: Colorado River below Yuma main canal
Shuttle: 5.5 miles, pavement and gravel
Best Season: Anytime
Peak Flow: post-dam—45,000 cfs, July 1983

By the time the Colorado River has reached Yuma, its water has been diverted, dammed, farmed, channeled, piped, filtered, polluted, and paddled upon by humans for the past several hundred miles. Still, the determined river keeps flowing onward in its inexorable push to mother ocean. It rarely makes it there these days, as our current state of human habitation dictates that we use all the water we can before it escapes back to the sea, or even Mexico for that matter.

Here in Yuma, however, the rio still has life, and it can provide a cool escape from the scorching heat of southwestern Arizona. The city of Yuma has shown new respect for the river environment in recent years, commissioning riverside restoration projects that return native plant species and biologically-rich floodplain wetlands to the Colorado corridor. The city recreation department even schedules float trips on the river, introducing youth to the natural wonders of their own backyard. The section of river that the locals float is described here.

The run starts at a notable geographical point for Arizona's river systems—the confluence of the Gila and Colorado. The put-in is actually on the timid and warm Gila, most of its water at this point being the result of surrounding agricultural runoff. Fifty yards away, the cold flowing Colorado courses by.

The river winds between walls of phragmites (river reeds), limiting your view to the sunken world of the river channel. Sounds of farming and suburban Yuma occasionally encroach from above, but they are distant distractions from the secluded channel. The current is slow but steady. In a few spots, eddies exist behind obstructions, providing opportunities for beginning paddlers to practice basic river running skills.

This stretch is mostly free of hazards, but there is one spot I noticed that was lethal. A couple miles into the run, three culverts sit just below water level on river right, sucking water down in small but powerful whirlpools that lead to the netherworld. Don't investigate too closely, and

Flatwater Rivers 17

Sand patterns on the lower Colorado

steer clear if you're swimming.

Just about when you see the first bridge spanning the river in town, look for a culvert diversion and short trail leading up on river left. This is access to the east wetlands channel, a newly restored floodplain that exists where the Gila confluence once was. The Gila was re-channeled to its current location in the 1930s, a period when the lower Colorado was initially tamed following the completion of Boulder Dam.

The river runs beneath a couple bridges as it enters downtown Yuma, and passes a park on river left. This is a possible take-out, but you may also continue another mile to West Wetlands Park. This is another river restoration project providing bird habitat and public access to the once-mighty Colorado.

Logistics: The take-out is at West Wetlands Park in Yuma. Take the Winterhaven exit off I-8, and go left, traveling south back across the river. At 1st Street, turn right (west), and follow it about a half mile to 12th Avenue. Turn right (north) on 12th, which leads 300 yards to the park along the river.

For the put-in, head back east on 1st street to 4th Avenue. Turn right (south) on 4th, and make a left at the first stoplight, which is Giss Parkway. Take Giss until you go under the freeway, then turn left uphill on Prison Hill Road. Follow Prison Hill a few hundred yards up the hill, and take a hard right onto an unsigned dirt canal road running along the south side of a canal known as the Salt Canal. Follow the Salt Canal road for 4.1 miles, turn left to cross over the canal, and head back west along the north side of the canal. In about a half mile, near where the canal bends from northwest to west, there is a spur road leading down to a beach area on the Gila just above its confluence with the Colorado. You are now at the put-in known locally as "Shit Creek." It is a trashed and renowned party spot. Leaving a fancy car here is not recommended.

Flatwater Rivers   19

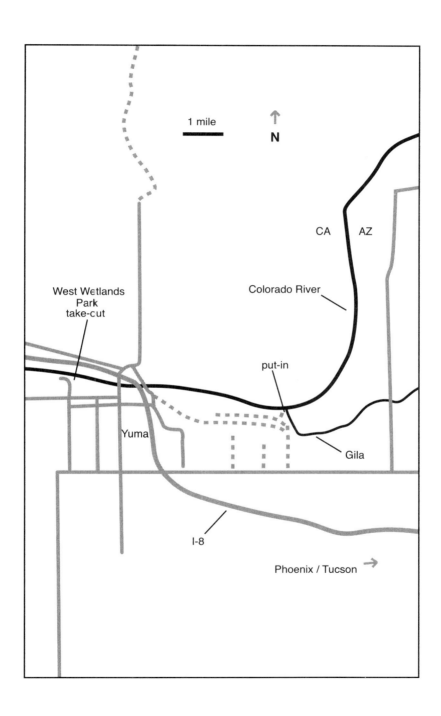

Glen Canyon

General Description: A river paddle in a scenic canyon.
Motorized Traffic: Moderate
Difficulty: Moderate if you float downstream only / Advanced to paddle upstream
Length: 15 miles
Gage: Colorado River at Lees Ferry
Shuttle: No driving shuttle / To arrange for a ride upstream, contact Colorado River Discovery in Page at 928-522-6644. Information on "backhauling" upstream to the dam can be found on their website: www.raftthecanyon.com. Shuttles are dependent on CRD's trip schedule, which runs roughly March through October.
Best Season: April — November
Peak Flow: pre-dam—300,000 cfs, July 7, 1884, post-dam—97,300 cfs, June 29, 1983

This is the section of the Colorado River upstream from Grand Canyon, but below Lake Powell and Glen Canyon Dam. Paddling here offers a glimpse of what the labyrinthine Glen Canyon was like before it was flooded by the reservoir.

Starting from Lees Ferry, there are two approaches to paddling this section. You can get a ride upstream with a motorboat, and float back down, or you can paddle upstream against the current, and float back down. Details for getting a ride upstream are listed above.

Paddling upstream is no problem in a fast touring kayak or sea kayak. There are eddylines and strong current, however, so those with no river experience will be challenged. Low water (less than 10,000 cfs) offers more eddies to aid in attainment, but also exposes constricted riffles of shallow fast water. Higher water (over 15,000 cfs) means a wider deeper channel, but there is riverwide current that requires vigorous paddling or even portaging in some spots.

The many fishermen who frequent this part of the Colorado have no problem with the current as they cruise along powered by large outboards. Because the warm muddy Colorado has been transformed into a cold clear river below the dam, the native fish have nearly been extirpated, but rainbow trout have thrived. This 15-mile stretch of river is one of the premier trout streams in the country.

Whether you have come to catch fish or not, this is a great flatwater float. The river winds between vertical walls of sandstone 1,200 feet high. In autumn, the cliffs burn orange in the sunlight. Following summer thunderstorms, the rims explode with spectacular flash flood waterfalls.

You can spend a full day here, or camp overnight. The campsites are

Navajo Sandstone walls dominate Glen Canyon

developed with toilets. In 2010, it was $31 for a permit to park a car and launch a boat at Lees Ferry, good for seven days. For more information, call Glen Canyon National Recreation Area at 928-608-6200.

Logistics: Take Highway 89A toward Marble Canyon, AZ, and turn down the paved Lees Ferry road. This turn is located a couple hundred yards beyond the Marble Canyon Bridge. Follow the Lees Ferry road to its end at the Lees Ferry launch ramp. There is a permit fee to park here. For the latest fees, call GCNRA at 928-608-6200.

Fisherman enjoying the clear post-dam waters of the Colorado

Flatwater Rivers 23

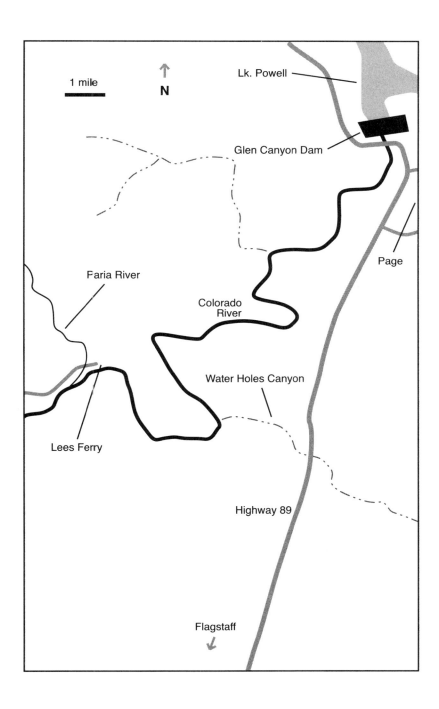

Topock Gorge

General Description: A section of the lower Colorado River in a scenic canyon
Motorized Traffic: Moderate / High
Difficulty: Easy
Length: 17 miles
Gage: Colorado River below Davis Dam
Shuttle: 30 miles, paved
Best Season: November — February
Peak Flow: pre-dam—300,000 cfs, July, 1884, post-dam—60,000 cfs, July, 1983

The Topock Gorge is not quite as intimidating as it might sound. There are no big rapids or gnashing rocks here, but there are dangers. A paddler's biggest fear on Topock Gorge will likely emanate from brightly-colored speeding boats that are usually titled with a word ending in the letters OR—Eliminator, Terminator, Dominator....The speedboats that skip across these waters are so amazingly fast and loud that paddlers will actually feel a kinship with any watercraft less than 30 feet in length and under 200 horsepower.

Come during mid-week in mid-winter, however, and you'll notice a dearth of the flashy cigarette boats. Even on some weekends in winter, Topock is relatively quiet, just a smooth flowing river between wetland marshes and craggy desert cliffs.

About four miles below the freeway, the river enters The Needles, a wild landscape of volcanic spires, narrow canyons, and rock arches. This could be a great area for a hike away from the river, or camping. Topock must be done as a day trip, however, as there is a camping restriction through this wildlife refuge. Below a sharp left turn called Devils Elbow (there is sometimes an eddyline here for practicing river skills), the terrain opens some, but picturesque rock formations still hover above shoreline.

The mountains relent at Blankenship Valley about 12 miles into the run, and the river broadens and slows. Extensive marshlands weave into the river channel, providing excellent bird habitat.

Fingers of marsh reaching into the flooded river channel can make navigation challenging as you near the take-out. Hopefully you checked your landmarks when driving shuttle, and you'll notice Castle Rock on the left. There is a sign on the river indicating this rock dome, where you will take a channel to the left that leads into the take-out cove at Castle Rock.

Logistics: For the take-out: From the stoplight on Highway 95 at the north end of Lake Havasu City, take London Bridge Road 0.7 miles to Fathom

Flatwater Rivers 25

Paddling into a tortured desert landscape at Topock

Road. Turn west on Fathom and follow it about a half mile to Reef Road. Go left on Reef for 1 block to Vista, and follow Vista to the right another quarter mile to a dirt road at the bottom of the valley that heads left. It is a couple hundred yards down the dirt road to a parking area. From here, it is a short walk to the water.

The put-in is reached by heading north on Highway 95 to I-40. Take I-40 west to exit #1—Golden Shores/Oatman. Head north from the exit a few hundred yards. Topock Marina is located just north of the railroad tracks that you'll drive under. It is $5 to launch a kayak or canoe at Topock Marina, and there is also access to a nice wetland area called Lost Lake from here.

Topock Gorge

Flatwater Rivers 27

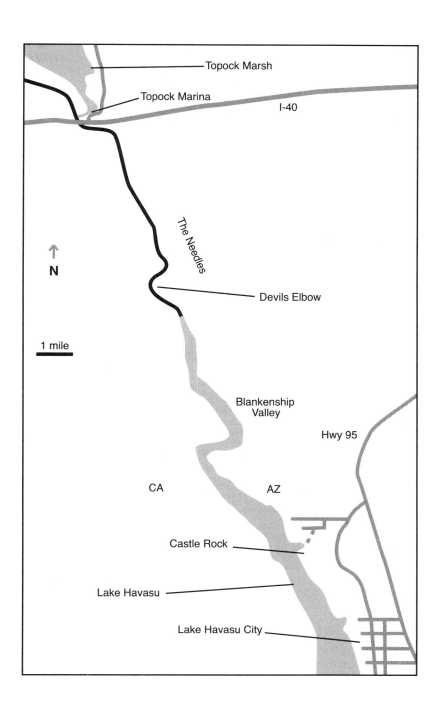

Lower Salt River
(Saguaro Lake to Granite Reef)

General Description: A popular section of the Salt River on the outskirts of Phoenix
Motorized Traffic: Low (none)
Difficulty: Advanced (class I—II whitewater)
Length: 10 miles
Flow: minimum: 300 cfs
   ideal: 500 — 1,500 cfs
Gage: Salt River below Stewart Mountain Dam
Shuttle: 7 miles, paved, hitchable
Best Season: This stretch is dependent on releases from Saguaro Lake. The most consistent flows tend to come between early May and mid-October. Below the confluence of the Verde, flows are often adequate for runs in winter.
Peak Flow: 64,000 cfs—February 16, 1980. *This is an average flow for that day.*

This is a heavily used stretch of river. In summer, the water can be nearly covered bank to bank with inner tubers escaping the city heat. It is a raucous place, a menagerie of party animals, police officers, beer cans, and boom boxes.

This is only the scene on summer weekends, however. Come to the lower Salt midweek, or in the off-season, and you will find a desert river flowing through a scenic, mostly natural setting. There are a number of class I riffles to usher you along, eddies to catch, and even an occasional surf wave or two for the aspiring whitewater paddler.

The farthest upstream one can find good public river access is Pebble Beach. Below here, the river gradually meanders away from the road for a few miles. Bluffs rise steeply from the water in places. Eagles, kingfishers, and herons fly over the cool clear river, and the Sonoran Desert comes to water's edge.

About 6 miles downstream from Pebble Beach, the Verde River enters on river right. During times of low water when there is minimal water being released from Stewart Mtn. Dam, the Verde often adds enough water to allow for a short run below here. Access to this spot is provided via the Phon Sutton Recreation Area.

There is a small rapid right at the confluence of the two major desert rivers. Beginners might be challenged here, but a portage on the left is easy. Class I water continues between pools, with a class II rapid coming in a right channel where an island splits the river. This is a good spot for beginning whitewater paddlers to practice eddy turns and ferry angles.

Flatwater Rivers 29

Enjoy ng a sunny day of river paddling on the outskirts of Phoenix

The last mile of the run mimics lake-like flatness before the Granite Reef take-out. The scenery remains pleasant in this last section, with the Four Peaks forming the skyline upstream, and Mt. McDowell as a backdrop to the north of the river. In winter, egrets and coots congregate on the water. The incoming flight path for Sky Harbor is directly overhead, however, reminding us that we are indeed on the fringe of a large city.

Logistics: Take Power Road north out of Mesa. This road turns into the Bush Highway, and first reaches the Salt River at the Granite Reef river access. From Granite Reef, it is 2.4 miles to the turn for Phon Sutton, 3.4 miles to the Coon Bluff turn, and 7.1 miles to Pebble Beach.

The dramatic Four Peaks rise in close proximity to the Lower Salt

Flatwater Rivers

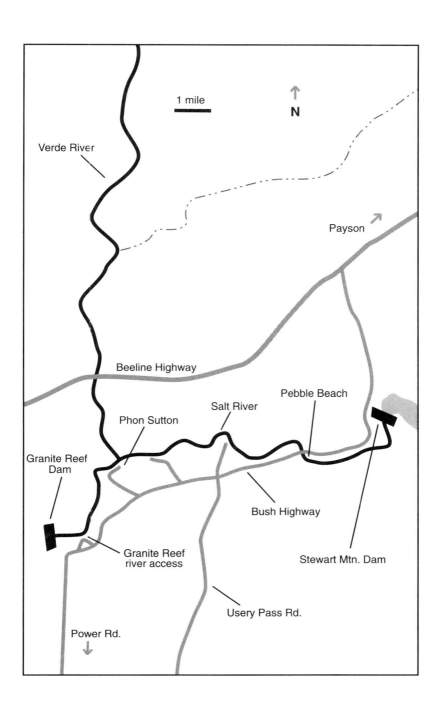

Gila River
(Kelvin run)

General Description: A flatwater desert river with summer flows, good current, and plentiful birdlife
Motorized Traffic: Low (none)
Difficulty: Advanced (class I—II whitewater)
Length: 12 miles
Flow: minimum: 200 cfs
ideal: 300 — 700 cfs
Gage: Gila River at Kelvin
Shuttle: 29 miles, mostly good dirt road
Best Season: May through September. Flows here come from releases at Coolidge Dam 40 miles upstream. When the reservoir is low or empty during droughts, releases will be small or non-existent. When there is available water, the release is for summer agriculture.
Peak Flow: Pre-dam: 190,000 cfs, November 28, 1905 / Post-dam: 100,000 cfs, October 2, 1983.

Singing the low-water blues during an Arizona June? This could be your salvation. After all the free flowing rivers in the Grand Canyon state have trickled down to creeks that will barely float a beer can, this stretch of the Gila often holds boatable flows. Irrigation in the desert lowlands dictates that San Carlos Reservoir releases the water it has gathered during the previous rainy season. The result is a flowing river when most Arizona streams are only memories.

This section of the Gila runs through a final range of rugged mountains before spilling out onto the flatlands near Florence. Although there are steep slopes of granite adjacent to the river for much of this run, the river itself belies the gnarled surroundings, running placidly beneath a forested floodplain.

There are no real rapids, but a steady current requires paddlers to remain attentive. Numerous live and dead strainers penetrate the channel, and a few places demand well-timed ferries in order to have a clean line. The current is not very pushy except at high water, so beginning whitewater paddlers should be able to make this run if accompanied by an experienced leader. Still, there is potential for disaster in a couple spots, and anyone floating here must be aware that getting snagged on an overhanging tree in fast current is a dangerous situation.

When you're not dodging the trees, there is plenty of scenery and wildlife to enjoy. Surrounding the river is a riparian forest of tamarisk, willow, and cottonwood. Numerous birds call this micro jungle habitat home, and even novice birders are likely to see some interesting avian critters. On

Flatwater Rivers 33

Sonoran Desert paddling on the Gila in June

our trip, we spotted bright vermilion flycatchers, black hawks, sharp shinned hawks, a great horned owl, and a golden eagle. Juxtaposed above the green river corridor is a hot and dry Sonoran Desert landscape.

Immediately below the Kelvin put-in, the river cuts through a small mountain range before passing a ranch and emerging into a valley, where it meanders for a few miles. The Gila then enters another short canyon. Upon exiting the second canyon, the take-out seems near as the terrain opens and several railroad access points are visible from the water. Trip's end, however, is still a few miles distant as the river nears yet more rugged mountains.

Logistics: From Florence, take the Florence/Kelvin Highway east. In about 10 miles, the road turns to graded dirt. In 5.8 more miles, turn left on Cochron Road near a linear formation of granite boulders. It is about 13 miles down Cochron Road to the river. There are a couple sandy spots en route, but our Honda Civic made it. You'll have to cross the railroad tracks and follow a two-track through a tunnel of tamarisk to reach a beach at the river.

For the put-in, return to the Kelvin/Florence Highway, and continue east for about 16 miles. Just before crossing the bridge over the Gila, turn right on Riverside Road, and follow it upstream about a quarter mile to a small riverside pull-out that serves as the put-in.

Flatwater Rivers

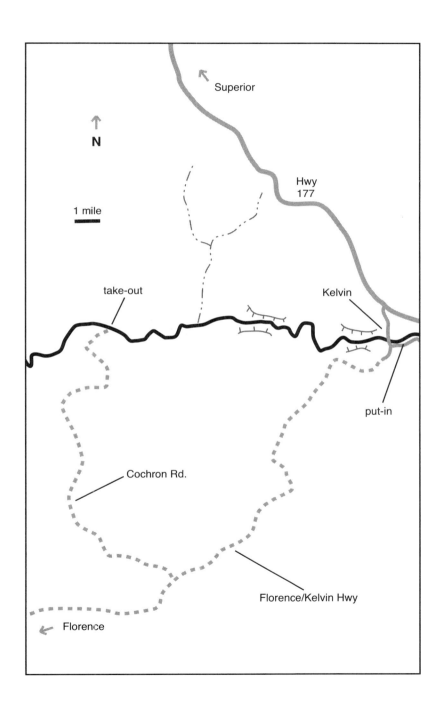

DESERT LAKES

Lake Powell

General Description: A huge reservoir in spectacular slickrock desert
Motorized Traffic: Moderate
Surface Area When Full: 170,294 acres
Shoreline When Full: 1,960 miles
Fish Species: largemouth bass, smallmouth bass, striped bass, crappie, sunfish, channel catfish, walleye
Elevation: 3,600'
Best Season: May, September, October, November

Reviled, revered, and recreated upon, Lake Powell means many things to many people. Formed in 1963 with the completion of Glen Canyon Dam, Lake Powell is a huge body of blue water in an otherwise water-less landscape of sandstone desert. Across the lake's surface rumbles giant houseboats, ski boats, personal watercraft, and touring kayaks and canoes, the occupants contentedly enjoying a liquid playground amidst a scorched inhospitable land of rock. The scene is quintessentially surreal.

Paddling here can be great fun. There are innumerable canyons, bays, and inlets to explore, and hiking beyond the shoreline reveals a vast wondrous landscape. The lake is busy in summer, but even then it is a big enough place to escape the crowds with some effort. There are many lake arms containing passageways too narrow for big boats, allowing only kayaks and canoes (and an occasional jet-ski) to proceed.

Getting up the lake to explore these many side canyons can be laborious. When the lake is low, as it is likely to be for the foreseeable future, every boat launching from the southern shore must travel the same narrow channel for the first several miles. For paddlers, this means struggling through wake waves and crowds until reaching more open waters. The open water, big views, good camping, and general Lake Powell attractions begin around Labyrinth Canyon about 10 miles from the Antelope Point access.

One strategy that would limit your time spent battling the bothersome entrance channel is to hire a ride for this first part. Hopping on a motorboat for the first part of a paddling trip might seem antithetical to the experience for some, but if your focus is purely pleasure, then you won't be missing much by hitching a ride through the access channel.

Once onto the main lake body, the exploration options are virtually limitless. Lake Powell stretches for 186 miles in length, with a side canyon entering every few miles. At least a few days are needed to get a real sense of this place, and a week or more is preferable.

If you are short on time, I recommend launching from Wahweap or Lone Rock on Wahweap Bay, and paddling across the bay for a day of pad-

Desert Lakes 39

Lake Powell — the perfect film location for *Planet of the Apes*

dling or a night of camping.

Wherever you go, and whatever your opinion about Lake Powell (beautiful enhancement of nature, or destroyer of Glen Canyon?, or as Ed Abbey said: "a 180-mile sewer lagoon"), this is a paddling destination not to be missed.

Logistics: There are two Arizona launch points for Lake Powell: Wahweap and Antelope Point. An entrance fee to Glen Canyon National Recreation Area is required to use either of these ramps, or any lake access for that matter. Antelope Point is the best launch point for reaching the upper lake unless the water level is medium to high and the shortcut north of Antelope Island is open.

To reach Antelope Point, take Highway 98 out of Page, toward Kayenta and the power plant. Just past mp 299, take a left toward Antelope Point. In about 4 miles, you will come to the GCNRA entrance station. The launch ramp is another mile straight ahead.

To reach Wahweap, cross the Colorado River on Highway 89 and continue 0.7 miles to the signed turn for Wahweap Marina. Pass through the GCNRA entrance station, and follow signs for the launch ramp, about another two miles down the road.

Lone Rock Beach can sometimes offer a less crowded launch area. To get there, continue on Highway 89 past the Wahweap turn. In several miles you will cross the Utah state line. Shortly after entering Utah, turn right on Lone Rock Road, and follow this paved, then dirt road about two miles to the water.

For an even more secluded launch area, check out Warm Creek Bay. This is found by turning off Highway 89 at Big Water about 7 miles into Utah. It is 12 miles down this dirt (axle-deep car sticking mud when wet) road to Warm Creek Bay. Getting to the water here when the lake is low can involve extensive boat dragging.

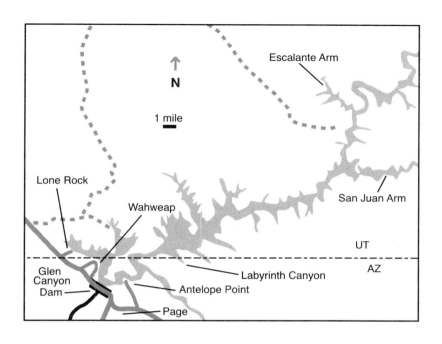

Lake Mead

General Description: A huge reservoir in Great Basin desert
Motorized Traffic: Moderate / High
Surface Area When Full: 157,900 acres
Shoreline When Full: 550 miles
Fish Species: largemouth bass, striped bass, channel catfish, sunfish, crappie
Elevation: 1,221' when full
Best Season: September — November, February, March

Lake Mead is a huge waterway. At more than 100 miles in length and surface water exceeding 150,000 acres, Mead was once the largest man-made lake in the world, and still ranks high as one of the country's biggest reservoirs.

Lake Mead was created in 1935 with the completion of Boulder Dam, which was later renamed Hoover Dam by a president named not too ironically, Hoover. The dam was, and still is, a marvel of engineering, containing enough concrete to make a highway from Seattle to Miami. At the time of its construction, it was the tallest dam in the world.

All that concrete of course serves as a plug to the temporarily subdued Colorado River. The river flow has not kept pace with the rate of water usage in recent years, so the reservoir has shrunk dramatically. Even since research for this book was begun several years ago, the lake has diminished dramatically.

The easternmost launch point on the lake, Pearce Ferry, was once a favorite starting location for kayaks, offering access to the lowest reaches of Grand Canyon. Now Pearce Ferry is a ghost ramp with barely a drop of water in sight. Two miles from the now closed ramp, the muddy Colorado drifts along hidden beneath steep banks, forging a new channel through lake sediments.

Lake Mead might be smaller than it once was, but there are still miles upon miles of open water and desert inlets to explore here. Most of the motorboat traffic launches from marinas on the north side of the lake in Nevada. The most secluded areas of the lake are located on the upper end of the Colorado arm. The Iceberg Canyon region offers dramatic views of stark mountains rising in geologic plates out of the lake waters. There are plenty of places to hike off into lonely desert country here.

The best launch point for this eastern end of the lake is South Cove, a wide concrete ramp near the community of Meadview. Temple Bar is a little farther down the lake, and this small lake town offers a marina, a cafe, and a more centralized location for exploring up or down the lake.

Heading north along the Arizona shoreline from Temple Bar will reveal a

Desert Lakes   **43**

Fully supported kayak-tripping on Lake Mead

wealth of coves and beaches to explore. If you are near Hoover Dam and wish to go paddling in that area, Kingman Wash is your best bet for low-key access to the water. This dirt "ramp" is only a few miles from the dam. Castle Cove, a favorite destination among paddlers, is accessible from here. Wherever you launch from, Lake Mead can provide everything from a quick float to a multi-day tour.

Winds can get very strong on this broad desert reservoir, so approach any open water crossings with a keen eye on the weather and a readiness to deal with big choppy water.

Logistics: South Cove is located about 8 miles past Meadview, AZ. From Kingman, take Highway 93 about 30 miles northwest to a sign for Meadview / Pearce Ferry at county road #25. It is about 46 miles down this paved road to the South Cove ramp.

For Temple Bar, take Highway 93 northwest from Kingman about 52 miles. Turn right near milepost 20, following signs for Temple Bar. It is about 28 miles from Highway 93 to Temple Bar.

The turn for Kingman Wash is located about 3 miles southeast from Hoover Dam on Highway 93. It is another 3.5 miles down a dirt road from here to the lake.

For more information on Lake Mead paddling, check out www.kayaklakemead.com.

Desert Lakes 45

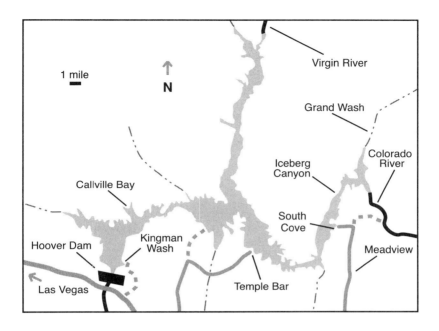

McHood Park Lake
(Clear Creek Reservoir)

General Description: A small recreational reservoir set in a sandstone canyon
Motorized Traffic: Low
Surface Area When Full: 85 acres
Shoreline When Full: 4.1 miles
Fish Species: brown trout, rainbow trout
Elevation: 4,860'
Best Season: April — October

This is the closest thing to Lake Powell south of the Utah line. The lake fills the lower end of the East Clear Creek canyon, twisting between narrow sheer cliffs of Coconino Sandstone.

The launch area is below the narrows of the upper lake. Here you will find a small but open body of water adjacent to a paved parking lot and shade ramadas. If you choose to paddle the lower end of the lake, beware of a swirling whirlpool near the dam that sucks water underground before discharging back into the bed of East Clear Creek. The no swimming signs in this area mean business.

The upper end of the lake is generally the most attractive area for paddlers to explore. Here the smooth lake water curves beneath sculpted rock faces. If you paddle far enough, you will reach the shallows at the mouth of East Clear Creek. Small light boats can be dragged upstream a short ways to reach a long pool on the creek that offers yet more paddling. There is plentiful poison ivy in the shady canyon bottom, so avoid the green stuff!

Logistics: From Winslow, take Highway 87 south about a mile and turn east on Route 99. In 4.4 miles you'll arrive at McHood Park Lake, with parking and launch areas on the east shoreline.

Desert Lakes 47

Sheer canyon walls border McHood Park Lake.

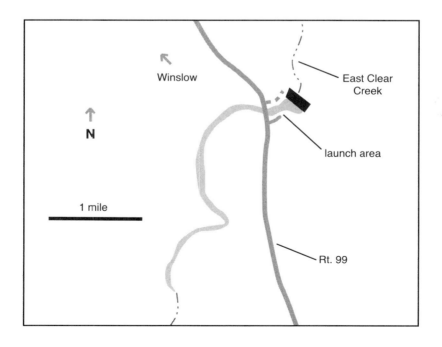

Lake Pleasant

General Description: A large reservoir north of Phoenix
Motorized Traffic: Moderate to High
Surface Area When Full: 7,500 acres
Shoreline When Full: 114 miles
Fish Species: largemouth bass, white bass, striped bass, crappie, sunfish, channel catfish, flathead catfish, carp
Elevation: 1,700'
Best Season: November — March

Lake Pleasant is a large reservoir on the Agua Fria River not far from the Valley of the Sun. It is a popular destination for ski boats, jet boats, house boats, jet skis, wave runners, you name it. Fortunately, it is a big enough body of water to allow escape from the traffic, and in the off season it is a pretty quiet place.

The Bradshaw and Hieroglyphic Mountains provide a rugged and scenic backdrop along the northern shores of the lake. To the south, the Valley looms. No-wake zones on the upper arms of the lake offer more quiet paddling opportunities. You are likely to see turtles, grebes, ducks, and herons here. A short walk away from the water will have you in saguaro-rich Sonoran Desert.

Logistics: Head north from Phoenix on I-17 to exit 223—the Carefree Highway. Contrary to logic, do not turn onto Lake Pleasant Road, which you will reach in about 6 miles from the freeway. Rather, continue another half mile and turn right toward Pleasant Harbor if you want to use the private marina. Entry here is $6 with or without a boat.

For the county access, continue west on Highway 74, cross the Agua Fria River (the watercourse which forms Pleasant), and turn right onto Castle Creek Road near milepost 19. In 2.5 miles down Castle Creek Road, there is a signed turn leading to the lake and Waddell Dam Visitor Center. Daily fees to Lake Pleasant Regional Park are $5 per vehicle and $2 per watercraft.

There is one more launch ramp farther up the lake. This is reached by traveling another 3.5 miles up Castle Creek Road and turning right at the stop. This ramp is also part of the Lake Pleasant Regional Park, and fees apply.

Desert Lakes   **49**

Having a Pleasant day

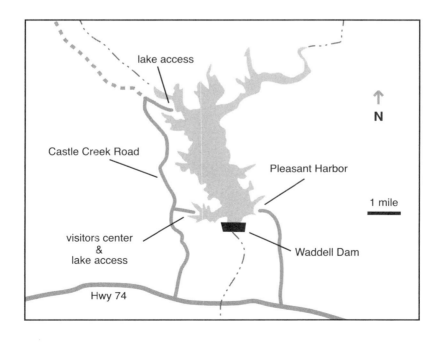

Horseshoe Reservoir

General Description: A fluctuating reservoir on the Verde River
Motorized Traffic: Low
Surface Area When Full: 2,800 acres
Shoreline When Full: 27 miles
Fish Species: largemouth bass, smallmouth bass, crappie, sunfish, channel catfish, flathead catfish, carp
Elevation: 1,950'
Best Season: February — June

In order to serve as a water collection basin and alleviate flooding downstream, Horseshoe Reservoir is kept empty much of the time. Don't expect to find a big blue lake here. A narrow muddy channel of the Verde River winding across an empty lake bed is a more typical scene.

When the lake is full, however, one can paddle 5 miles across the open waters to the last few turns of the wild and scenic Verde River. There are a scarcity of protected coves on this reservoir, but due to motor restrictions (no water skiing or personal watercraft), whatever shoreline you might choose to explore will likely be more quiet than other nearby reservoirs.

Logistics: From Cave Creek, AZ, take Cave Creek Road northeast to Bartlett Dam Road. Follow Bartlett Dam Road for 6.3 miles, and turn north onto Horseshoe Dam Road (road #205). It is 11 miles from here to the launch ramp at Horseshoe Reservoir. The first 2 miles of Horseshoe Dam Road are paved, then it is graded dirt.

Desert Lakes 51

Changes aren't permanent....   ....but Change is

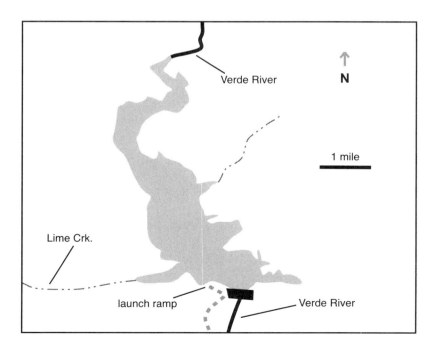

Bartlett Lake

General Description: A popular and scenic desert reservoir near Phoenix
Motorized Traffic: High
Surface Area When Full: 2,000 acres
Shoreline When Full: 33 miles
Fish Species: largemouth bass, crappie, sunfish, channel catfish, flathead catfish, carp
Elevation: 1,790'
Best Season: November — March

Bartlett Lake is on par with Saguaro and Canyon Lakes when it comes to summer crowding. There is a limit to the number of boats allowed on the water at once, so on weekends this place can literally be sold out. During winter, however, it is often pretty quiet.

There are many quaint coves along the lake shore, but few real arms to explore. The main upstream arm of the lake is the one exception. Water skiing is restricted here, which slows the speedboat factor somewhat, making it an attractive area for paddling.

Along parts of the lake, there are low cliffs of neon-colored tuff—the same formation which is prominent in the Superstition Mountains to the southeast. Beyond the eastern shoreline of Bartlett lies the rugged and wild countryside surrounding the Mazatzal Range.

Logistics: From Cave Creek, AZ, take Cave Creek Road (#24) northeast to Bartlett Dam Road. Follow the paved Bartlett Dam Road for 13.5 miles to the lake and marina. For the upper end of the lake, turn left before reaching the bottom of the hill, and follow signs 3.7 miles to Bartlett Flat. There is a $6 per vehicle fee, and a $4 fee for launching a boat.

Desert Lakes 53

Inspecting formations of tuff along Bartlett Lake

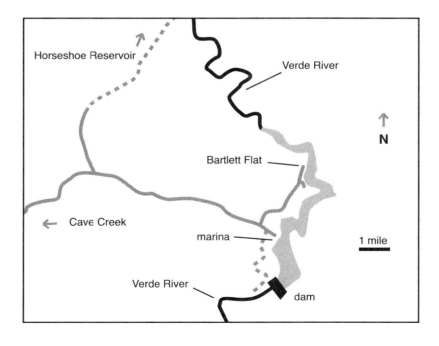

Roosevelt Lake

General Description: A big reservoir less than two hours from Phoenix
Motorized Traffic: High
Surface Area When Full: 21,500 acres
Shoreline When Full: 128 miles
Fish Species: largemouth bass, smallmouth bass, crappie, sunfish, channel catfish, flathead catfish, carp, bluegill
Elevation: 2,148'
Best Season: October — April (Tonto Creek arm is closed from November 15 to February 15 for wildlife protection.)

Roosevelt Lake is big. Stretching over 20 miles in length across the Tonto Basin, Roosevelt is the largest and farthest upstream reservoir on the Salt River.

The mighty Salt is the primary source stream for Roosevelt, but Tonto Creek also adds significant water from the western end of the basin. This western arm of the lake is home to a swamp of cottonwood and willow trees, creating an interesting setting for paddling when the lake is full.

There is plenty of open water on Roosevelt too, making it a favorite for speedboat enthusiasts. You will rarely have Roosevelt to yourself, and secluded campsites are hard to find, but Roosevelt (named for Teddy, not FDR) is in an undeniably dramatic setting between the Four Peaks and the Sierra Anchas. And if marathon paddling is your thing, there is enough lake here to paddle until your palms are blistered.

Logistics: Take Highway 87 north from Scottsdale about 50 miles, and turn southeast on Highway 188. It is about 25 miles from here to the western end of the lake. Most of the launch sites require a $6 fee for use.

Desert Lakes 55

Kayak-fishing on Roosevelt

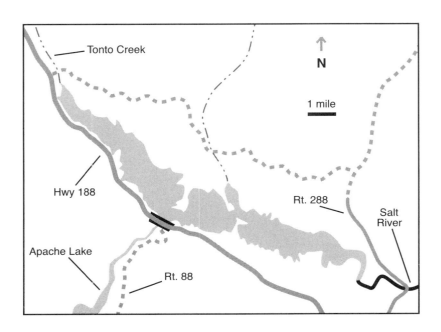

Apache Lake

General Description: A Salt River reservoir in a relatively remote mountainous region
Motorized Traffic: Moderate / High
Surface Area When Full: 2,200 acres
Shoreline When Full: 43 miles
Fish Species: rainbow trout, largemouth bass, smallmouth bass, yellow bass, crappie, sunfish, channel catfish, flathead catfish, walleye, carp, bluegill
Elevation: 1,891'
Best Season: October — March

Apache Lake, accessible only by a narrow but well-maintained dirt road, is the least crowded of the Salt River reservoirs. The scenery can be stunning in evening light, and the country surrounding the lake is empty and wild.

A hotel, restaurant, and marina form the core of a tiny lake community on the south shore, and during summer weekends this can be a bustling place. In the off-season it is significantly mellower, however, and the lake can serve as a great vehicle to get into the adjacent wilderness. There are several nice coves providing excellent camping along the lake. The eastern end of the lake is a narrow channel leading to Roosevelt Dam, while the western portion of the lake is mostly open water ringed by dramatic cliffs of lichen-draped tuff—a compressed volcanic ash deposit.

Logistics: From Apache Junction, take Route 88 into the Superstition Mountains. It is about 33 miles from Apache Junction to the turn down road #79 for Apache Lake. From here (mp 229.3), it is almost a mile downhill to the Apache Lake Marina and Resort. Veer left for the Crabtree Wash Recreation Site launch area. There is a $6 per vehicle fee here, and $4 fee per watercraft.

Desert Lakes 57

The Painted Cliffs of Apache Lake

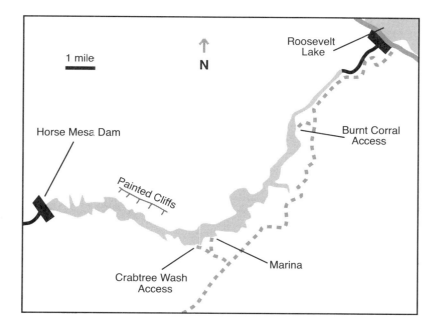

Canyon Lake

General Description: A popular lake in the Superstition Mountains
Motorized Traffic: High
Surface Area When Full: 970 acres
Shoreline When Full: 28 miles
Fish Species: rainbow trout, largemouth bass, yellow bass, sunfish, channel catfish, walleye, carp
Elevation: 1,660'
Best Season: November — March

Canyon Lake is just that. This reservoir winds through a narrow gorge in the heart of the tortured landscape of the Superstition Range. First time visitors will likely not even recognize the narrow portal which leads to the majority of this waterway. Rather, their initial impression will be that of an open bay set in a basin of desert mountains. This broad lower body of Canyon Lake is home to several launch sites, a marina, and restaurant.

For a short half day excursion, paddlers might want to explore the First Water or La Barge arms. Both lead to interesting hikes into rugged canyons, and the La Barge arm is closed to motors.

If you have a full day or more, the narrow main arm of Canyon Lake leads to several hidden coves tucked beneath dramatic cliffs. Blue Tank Canyon, located 5.5 miles up the lake, is the largest drainage on the north shore. A short hike here leads to shady canyon narrows.

Logistics: From Phoenix, take Highway 60 east to Apache Junction and exit at Idaho Road—exit 196. Follow Idaho Road north a couple miles and turn east onto Highway 88. Follow Highway 88 for 14.5 winding miles to Canyon Lake. There is a $6 fee per vehicle, and $4 fee per watercraft to paddle here.

Desert Lakes 59

Canyon Lake in the Superstition Mountains

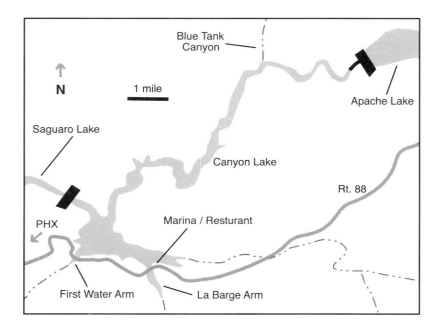

Saguaro Lake

General Description: A popular reservoir on the Salt River near Phoenix
Motorized Traffic: High
Surface Area When Full: 923 acres
Shoreline When Full: 23 miles
Fish Species: rainbow trout, largemouth bass, smallmouth bass, yellow bass, crappie, sunfish, channel catfish, walleye, carp
Elevation: 1,500'
Best Season: November — March

This is the final reservoir on the Salt River above the Phoenix metropolitan area. Being the closest SRP lake to the Valley of the Sun, Saguaro sees heavy traffic, and the launch area reflects this fact. A sheriff station is located here, along with a marina, store, and restaurant. On weekends during high season, the lake sees so much traffic that additional boats beyond a determined maximum number are not allowed on the water.

Despite the heavy use, there are some reasonable paddling options here. In fact, the bay at Butcher Jones Beach on the north shore is closed to motorized watercraft. The eastern end of the lake is a permanent no wake zone confined to a shady canyon. By paddling up the lake an hour or so, paddlers can penetrate this final narrow and rugged gorge of the Salt River cutting through the Superstition Mountains.

Logistics: Take Power Road north out of Mesa, AZ. This road turns into the Bush Highway, which follows the Salt River upstream for 10.6 miles to the access road for Saguaro Lake. The route is well signed. There is a $6 fee per vehicle, and $4 fee per watercraft to paddle here.

Desert Lakes 61

Where Saguaro Lake ends, the Salt River resumes.

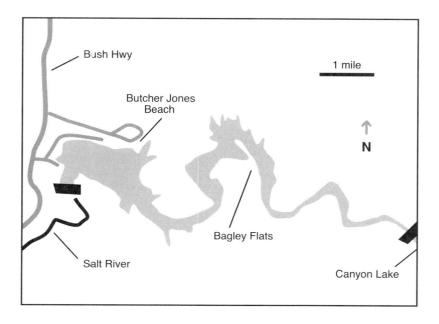

Tempe Town Lake

General Description: A park and lake on a controlled section of the Salt River in Tempe
Motorized Traffic: Low
Surface Area When Full: 220 acres
Shoreline When Full: 5 miles
Fish Species: rainbow trout (winter only), largemouth bass, channel catfish, sunfish
Elevation: 1,300'
Best Season: Anytime

This is a great little water getaway right in the center of metro Phoenix. Actually, the lake is in Tempe, at a spot on the Salt River that has served as a crossing for centuries.

Today this part of the Salt is a concrete and sand enclosed lake between two control dams on the normally dry river. The lake is a good two miles long, providing ample opportunity for rowing, fishing, paddle boating, canoeing, and kayaking. The water can get busy at times, but it is often a peaceful paddling locale amidst the breakneck traffic of the Valley.

Logistics: Take Mill Avenue to Curry Road and head east 100 yards to Lakeview Drive, which leads to the water.

Desert Lakes **63**

Tempe Town Lake—a convenient urban waterway

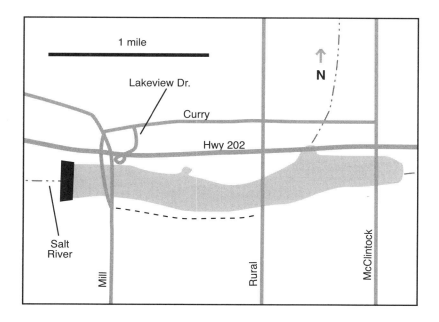

San Carlos Reservoir

General Description: A large desert reservoir in southeastern Arizona
Motorized Traffic: Moderate / High
Surface Area When Full: 8,480 acres
Shoreline When Full: 57 miles
Fish Species: bluegill, sunfish, channel catfish, flathead catfish, largemouth bass, crappie
Elevation: 2,700'
Best Season: March, April, September, October, November

This is a big reservoir with smaller crowds than Roosevelt or Pleasant—the other two big desert reservoirs in southern Arizona. Stark desert mountains form the skyline in all directions, and gulls and pelicans skim the water. Paddling here can remind one of Bahia de Concepcion near Mulege', Mexico. For a desert paddling getaway, however, San Carlos Reservoir is alot closer than Baja.

There are a variety of dirt roads on both the north and south sides of the lake, some of which lead to secluded coves. The camping is less than spectacular, however, due to thickets of dead tamarisk that inhabit the bays below the high water line.

Motorized traffic is significant here in the summer, but in the off season there are many days with hardly a boat on the lake. The scarcity of traffic makes San Carlos a suitable destination for a two or three day tour, although the off-lake hiking is only mediocre.

Logistics: From Globe, take Highway 70 east for 19 miles to Route 170, which heads south to the lake. From the 70/170 junction, it is 13 miles to Coolidge Dam, but spur roads leading to shoreline camps begin in about 7 miles.

A permit from the San Carlos Apache tribe is required for lake use and camping. Permits for boating are $15 for the first day, then $10 for each consecutive day. Permits are available at the Wildlife and Recreation Office, or Basha's Supermarket, both in Peridot.

Desert Lakes 65

An evening paddle on San Carlos

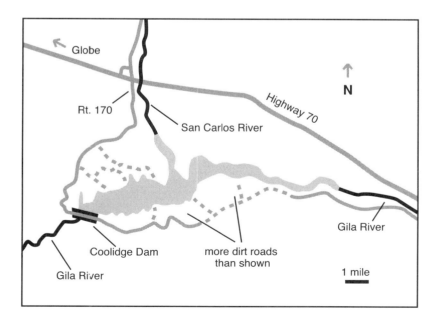

Topock Marsh

General Description: A backwater wetland along the Colorado River
Motorized Traffic: Low / Moderate
Surface Area When Full: 4,000 acres
Shoreline When Full: 23 miles
Fish Species: largemouth bass, striped bass, sunfish, crappie, tilapia, carp
Elevation: 500'
Best Season: November — March

Topock Marsh is an historical meander of the Colorado River. As the river was dredged and channelized, and the construction of Boulder Dam reduced floods, the marsh dried up. However, rebirth came to this rich wetland in 1966 when the south dike was built, returning waters to their natural flood channel. Now the water level in the marsh is controlled to mimic natural cycles. In the spring the water is highest. In autumn, the marsh is drawn down.

This is the time of year when Canadian snow geese arrive at Topock, fresh from their summer nests in the Arctic. We humans might follow the real snowbird's example, and flock here to enjoy the desert's winter sunshine. The marsh is big and maze-like. A full day or more could be spent exploring without seeing all the coves and inlets that snake through this huge marshland.

Logistics: Exit I-40 on the Arizona side of the river at exit #1 / Golden Shores / Oatman. Take Highway 95 north toward Bullhead City to reach several access sites. The first public launch area is Catfish Paradise 2.5 miles from the freeway. In another few miles, Highway 95 forks left at the community of Golden Shores. Two miles north of this junction is Five Mile Landing, a mobile home community with a small marina and launch ramps. The last access to the north end of the marsh is Pintail Slough, along the north dike. This is 5.3 miles north of the Highway 95 Golden Shores junction.

Desert Lakes 67

Topock Marsh along the Colorado River

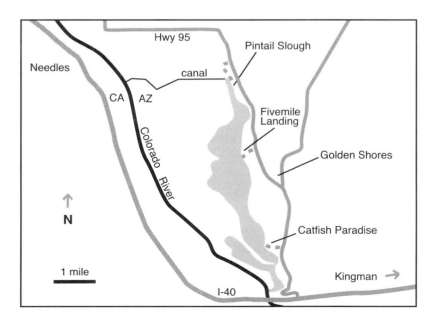

Bill Williams River Mouth

General Description: A wildlife refuge waterway in a riparian jungle
Motorized Traffic: Low
Surface Area When Full: Not applicable
Shoreline When Full: Not applicable
Fish Species: largemouth bass, striped bass, crappie, sunfish, channel catfish
Elevation: 450'
Best Season: October — March

The Havasu National Wildlife Refuge was created in 1941. Since then, 340 bird species have been spotted here. The mouth of the Bill Williams River is a good place to see some of those birds, as well as other riparian loving creatures like beaver.

The water you will be paddling on here is part of Lake Havasu. By paddling under the highway bridge, and up the Bill Williams River arm you can enter a world of rich wetlands. If you manage to portage a few beaver dams, you might even reach the modest Bill Williams River itself.

Most of the time, the "river" is a mere trickle flowing through a thick canopy of brush and trees. Following excessively wet periods, it is a big river, still flowing through a thick canopy of brush and trees.

Upstream on the Bill Williams, the Alamo Dam was constructed in 1966, reducing the huge floods that once cleared the Bill Williams River channel. The riparian jungle that exists at the river mouth today is similar, however, to the cottonwood forests that once lived along the banks of the Colorado.

Logistics: Travel Highway 95 north from Parker about 17 miles, or south from Lake Havasu City about 20 miles to mp 160.9. There is a launch area for the refuge here, located just south of the highway bridge over the Bill Williams River mouth. Be aware that there is a gate leading to the launch area that can be closed during early mornings or evenings.

Desert Lakes 69

This part of the Havasu National Wildlife Refuge offers top-notch birding.

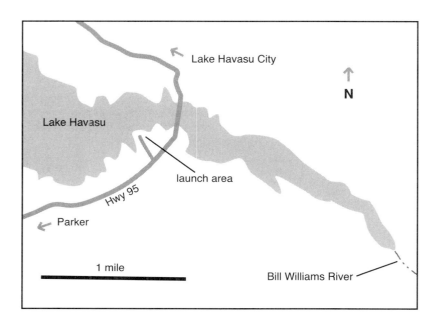

Martinez Lake

General Description: A partially developed oasis adjacent to the Colorado River
Motorized Traffic: Moderate
Surface Area When Full: 800 acres
Shoreline When Full: 9 miles
Fish Species: largemouth bass, smallmouth bass, striped bass, crappie, channel catfish, flathead catfish, tilapia, sunfish, carp, bullhead
Elevation: 200'
Best Season: November — March

Martinez Lake is a bird-rich waterway with a little bit of everything: narrow wetland channels, spacious open water, developed shorelines with houses, and secluded natural bays.

For a quick paddle into wildlife wetlands, hug the shoreline to the right after leaving the launch ramp, following the channel past a "no wake" buoy. If you are in search of a longer paddle session on open water, head through the next channel to the southeast that leads past homes and plentiful palm trees.

There are a few different species of palm here, making the swampy backwaters feel more like Florida's Everglades than Arizona's desert. Just as in Florida, you are likely to see pelicans and egrets here at Martinez Lake.

Logistics: Take Highway 95 north out of Yuma about twenty miles, and turn left on Martinez Lake Road between mileposts 46 and 47. It is about 10.5 miles along this undulating desert highway past the Yuma Proving Grounds to Red Cloud Mine Road. Take a right here, and veer right again in two miles toward the Imperial National Wildlife Refuge. In another mile, turn left at the refuge map/kiosk. Both the refuge visitor center and Meer's Point launch area are 0.5 and 0.9 miles farther, respectively.

Desert Lakes 71

Zooming in on wildlife at the Imperial N.W.R.

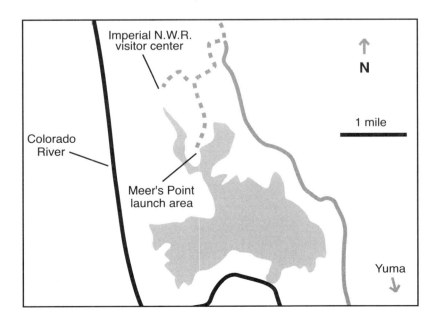

Mittry Lake

General Description: A wetland/lake near Yuma with extensive birdlife
Motorized Traffic: Moderate
Surface Area When Full: 550 acres
Shoreline When Full: 6.3 miles
Fish Species: largemouth bass, crappie, bullhead, channel catfish, flathead catfish, tilapia, sunfish, carp
Elevation: 185'
Best Season: November — March

Mittry Lake is a great place to pass the winter. Just ask the multiple RV campers along the south shoreline, or witness the large numbers of migratory birds that take up temporary residence here.

An upper arm of the lake is so rich with birdlife that it is known as "Teal Alley." This swampy northern end of the lake is closed to human visitation from November 15 to February 15 in order to provide a waterfowl sanctuary. Even with the closure, there is plenty of open water and marshland to explore here. Beyond the water-rich environment of the lake is the harsh landscape of the Laguna Mountains.

Logistics: Take Route 95 east in Yuma to Avenue 7E, where there is a sign for Mittry Lake. Turn north on 7E and follow it to Mittry Lake. Avenue 7E is paved for the first 9 miles, then turns to gravel for the last couple of miles past lakeside pull-outs to the launch ramp.

Desert Lakes 73

Winter paddling at Mittry Lake

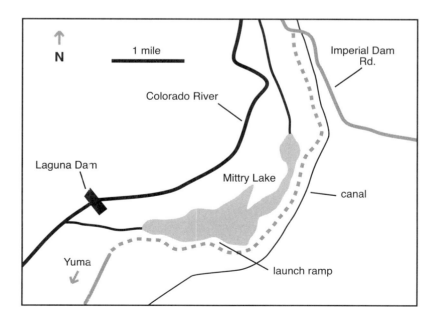

Patagonia Lake

General Description: A moderately-sized lake in southern Arizona with excellent bird watching
Motorized Traffic: Low / Moderate
Surface Area When Full: 231 acres
Shoreline When Full: 6.8 miles
Fish Species: rainbow trout, largemouth bass, crappie, sunfish, channel catfish, flathead catfish
Elevation: 3,800'
Best Season: March, April, October, November

Mt. Wrightson looms over Patagonia Lake.

One half of this lake is open to speedy motorboats, while a no-wake zone exists on the other end, so there is something here for everybody. This is a state park with a visitor center and an entrance fee.

Thickets of cattail grow along much of the shoreline, providing favorable habitat for the extensive bird life here. This is a top-notch birding locale, with over 275 species on the park checklist.

Grassy slopes of the Patagonia and Santa Rita foothills provide hiking opportunities adjacent to the lake, and 9,453-foot Mt. Wrightson is visible from the water. There are guided naturalist hikes along Sonoita Creek upstream from the lake which highlight the birds and butterflies of the area. Several developed campsites along the shoreline are only accessible by boat.

Logistics: Take AZ Route 82 northeast from Nogales or southwest from Patagonia to milepost 12, and turn onto the signed Patagonia Lake Road. It is 4 miles down this paved road to Patagonia Lake State Park.

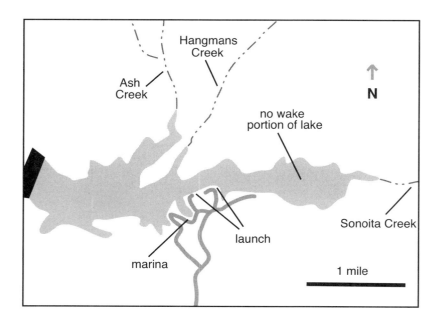

Pena Blanca Lake

General Description: A small quiet lake in far southern Arizona
Motorized Traffic: Low
Surface Area When Full: 51 acres
Shoreline When Full: 2.7 miles
Fish Species: rainbow trout, largemouth bass, sunfish, crappie, channel catfish *high mercury levels*
Elevation: 4,000'
Best Season: Anytime

White Pineapple Lake?

This is a true oasis in the rolling grasslands of southern Arizona. The water is clear and spring fed. The lake's stable water level leaves no unsightly bathtub ring that is common on many Arizona reservoirs.

Despite the natural appearance of Pena Blanca, it was formed in 1957 when an earthen dam was constructed. Since then, a plethora of riparian growth has taken foothold along the shoreline, providing excellent bird habitat. There are several fish species here too, but mercury levels have been found to be above EPA limits, so eating your catch isn't recommended.

The poisoned pescas are really the only blemish on this rich watering hole. Simply traveling to the scenic Atascosa Mountains that surround Pena Blanca is reward for this paddling excursion.

Logistics: Take the Ruby exit off I-19 about 12 miles north of Nogales. Head west on Highway 289 for about 10 miles to the lake.

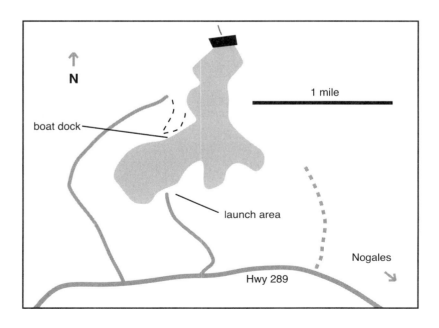

HIGH COUNTRY LAKES

Kaibab Lake

General Description: A small recreational reservoir near Williams
Motorized Traffic: Low / 8 hp max
Surface Area When Full: 61 acres
Shoreline When Full: 2.4 miles
Fish Species: rainbow trout, largemouth bass, sunfish, catfish
Elevation: 6,800'
Best Season: May — October

Kaibab Lake is an impoundment on Dogtown Wash, the same drainage that fills Dogtown Reservoir several miles upstream. Dogtown Wash is part of the Cataract Creek system—a massive basin that eventually culminates as the blue waters of Havasu Creek in the depths of Grand Canyon. The waters of Kaibab Lake rarely ever make it this far, except during times of flood when Kaibab Lake fills up and spills over as a small river flowing into the Cataract Creekbed.

During quieter times, Kaibab Lake hosts a scattering of fishermen along its banks, with most of the activity taking place adjacent to the campground, near the dam. The far end of the lake sees less traffic, but Highway 64 runs close by, creating significant noise from passing vehicles.

Although you might hear the highway, it is not visible from the lake, while the prominent mountains of the area are. Sitgreaves Mountain rises over the east end of the lake, and Bill Williams Mountain is visible to the south through the surrounding forest.

That forest is currently dominated by ponderosa pine, but it might not be for long. The lake is on the cusp of the juniper and scrub lands of northwestern Arizona. As global warming progresses, vegetative communities are shifting to accommodate the new climate regime. Locations on the margins of the ponderosa forest, such as Kaibab Lake, will likely be transformed into juniper-dominated settings in the future.

Logistics: Take Highway 64 north out of Williams. About 0.75 miles north of Interstate 40, turn left onto road #47 for Kaibab Lake. It is about a mile down this paved road to the campground and launch ramp on the shores of Kaibab Lake.

High Country Lakes 81

Kaibab is a Piute word for "mountain lying down."

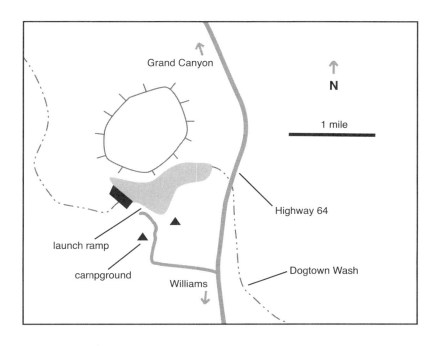

Dogtown Reservoir

General Description: A small lake in the forest near Williams
Motorized Traffic: Low / single electric motors only
Surface Area When Full: 70 acres
Shoreline When Full: 2 miles
Fish Species: rainbow trout, brown trout, largemouth bass, crappie, sunfish, catfish
Elevation: 7,100'
Best Season: May — October

Dogtown is a small lake in a pleasant pine and oak forest sitting at the foot of Bill Williams Mountain. Although it takes several miles of driving from the town of Williams to reach the lake, Dogtown is actually quite close to the city in air miles. Interstate 40 is nearby, and one can often hear the rumble of the railroad as it runs through the valley a couple miles from the lake.

An aqueduct from Dogtown runs to Williams for the town's water supply. Don't pollute the water.

Logistics: Head south out of Williams on Perkinsville Road (#173) for about 5 miles, and turn left onto forest road #140. Follow road #140 for 2.8 miles, and turn left onto road #132. Dogtown Reservoir is 0.7 miles farther. The route is signed well.

High Country Lakes 83

Cactus in bloom at Dogtown

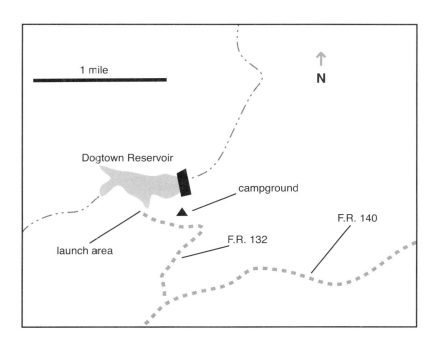

Lake Mary

General Description: Two lakes in the pines near Flagstaff with some development
Motorized Traffic: Moderate on upper lake / Low on lower lake
Surface Area When Full: 860 acres on upper lake
Shoreline When Full: 13 miles on upper lake
Fish Species: brown trout, rainbow trout
Elevation: 6,800'
Best Season: May — October

There are two lakes here: upper Lake Mary and lower Lake Mary. The upper lake is the more permanent of the two, as it is the first to catch runoff from Walnut Creek, the source for Lake Mary. If the upper lake fills completely and overflows the dam spillway, the lower lake will begin to fill. In dry spells, the lower lake is merely a meadow.

When it exists, the lower lake is the place to go if you want to avoid motors and do some fishing. Often the upper lake is busy with water skiers and sailboats. Upper Lake Mary is sometimes the only place to float a boat, however, and despite its popularity, it is worth a visit.

The best place to launch for paddlers is at the Narrows. Not far up-lake from this point, buoys warn motorized traffic of shallow water ahead. The lake is long and skinny and somewhat sheltered from the wind, but during strong springtime winds it still gets choppy. There are a few little sheltered coves to explore, views of the San Francisco Peaks, and sometimes elk grazing the shoreline in the evenings. Enjoy!

Logistics: Take Lake Mary Road (FH3) southeast from Flagstaff. It is about 5.5 miles to lower Lake Mary, and another 4 miles to the dam at upper Lake Mary. It is another 2 miles to the Narrows launch area. As of May, 2007, there is a $5 fee for day use at Lake Mary launch sites.

High Country Lakes 85

Upper and Lower Lake Mary after a big winter

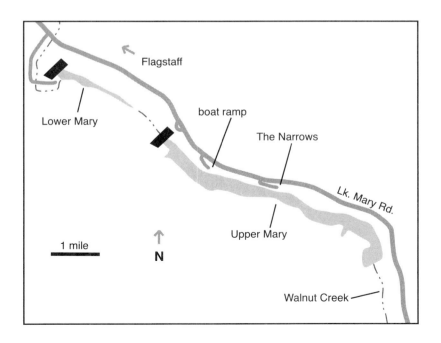

Ashurst Lake

General Description: A small, easily accessible lake with good birdlife
Motorized Traffic: Low / small lake with 8hp maximum
Surface Area When Full: 200 acres
Shoreline When Full: 3 miles
Fish Species: rainbow trout, channel catfish
Elevation: 7,100'
Best Season: April — November

Ashurst Lake is perched on the margin of the great ponderosa pine forests, where the wind-swept plains of northeastern Arizona meet the woodlands of the Mogollon Plateau. This unique location is easily reached via paved road, a convenience that makes it a popular watering hole on summer weekends.

The majority of weekenders that flock here are under-educated about backcountry ethics, and the polluted beaches of the lake bear evidence of their carelessness. However, once you get beyond the black mud, discarded beer cans, tangles of fishing line, bottle caps, and occasional wafts of human waste that grace the shoreline, paddling the open water of the lake can be surprisingly pleasant.

Birdlife is sometimes diverse and abundant here. Bald eagles and ospreys frequent the skies above, while egrets and ibises fish the weedy shallows. Watching these exotic-looking birds go about their daily business of survival makes the bustle of the nearby campground seem distant and unconnected.

During less popular periods (midweek, spring and fall), a real feeling of isolation is possible. The maximum 8hp regulation keeps big boats off the water, so even on busy weekends the lake is the domain of float tubes, kayaks, inflatables, and canoes. Overall, Ashurst offers easy access, nice scenery, and a pleasant, simple paddling experience.

Logistics: From Flagstaff, take Lake Mary Rd. (Forest Rd. #3) approximately 18.5 miles, and turn left on road #82E. This is just past mp 327. Paved road 82E leads 3.8 miles to Ashurst Lake. The launch area is to the right of the stop sign.

High Country Lakes 87

Monsoon season at Ashurst Lake

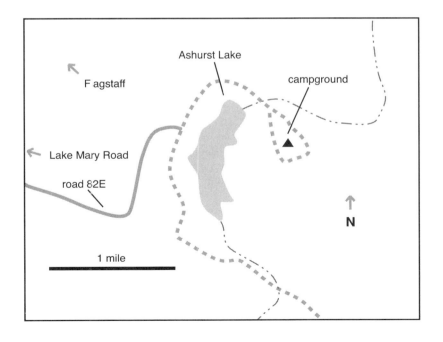

Kinnickinnick Lake

General Description: A semi-isolated small to medium sized lake
Motorized Traffic: Low / 8hp maximum
Surface Area When Full: 114 acres
Shoreline When Full: 2 miles
Fish Species: rainbow trout, channel catfish
Elevation: 7,000'
Best Season: May — October

Kinnickinnick Lake is an out-of-the-way body of water in northern Arizona. It is located on the dry northeastern slope of the Mogollon Plateau, so despite its 7,000 foot elevation, Kinnickinnick's surroundings are pygmy juniper forest.

Without the encroach of towering pines, good views of the nearby high country can be had from the open waters of the lake. The closest high point is Hutch Mountain at 8,532 feet. Farther north, Mormon Mountain (8,450 feet) is visible. Forty miles to the northwest, Arizona's highest mountains—the 12,633 foot high San Francisco Peaks—can be seen.

Besides the scenery, Kinnickinnick is home to waterfowl and stocked fish. Ospreys are frequent visitors to the lake, along with occasional Western Grebes, and of course the ubiquitous Great Blue Herons. Beneath the surface, trout share these waters with catfish, some of which can attain impressive size.

Good fishing is sometimes found near the east end of the lake, where a basalt earthen dam impounds the water creating the lake. In periods of high water, Kinnickinnick's overflow feeds into a smaller basin beyond the dam known as Morton Lake. If water makes it past here, it flows down Grapevine Canyon into Canyon Diablo, and then into the Little Colorado River.

If the water is high enough to make this journey, getting to Kinnickinnick might be tough. The 9-mile drive into the lake is on dirt roads that become mud bogs when wet. It is these rough roads that are Kinnickinnick's blessing however, making it a relatively quiet and relaxing refuge off the beaten path.

Logistics: From Flagstaff, take Lake Mary Road (FH #3) southeast for approximately 26 miles to milepost 319.5, where road #125 intersects the pavement. Take this dirt road northeast for 5 miles to an intersection, and turn right, or south, onto road #82. In 4 more miles, fork left to Kinnickinnick Lake, which is 0.5 miles farther

High Country Lakes   89

Kinnickinnick and Morton Lakes (the dark one) of northern Arizona

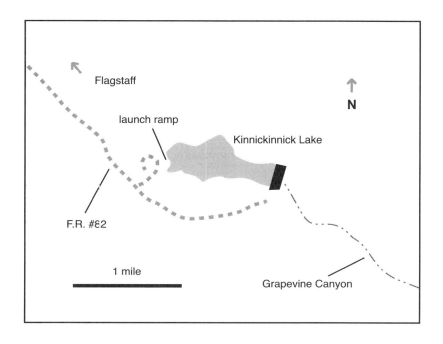

Stoneman Lake

General Description: A natural shallow lake in the pines
Motorized Traffic: Low / The lake is too shallow for most motors.
Surface Area When Full: 125 acres
Shoreline When Full: 2 miles
Fish Species: northern pike, yellow perch
Elevation: 6,700'
Best Season: May — November

This is Arizona's Crater Lake. Like its distant cousin in Oregon, Stoneman Lake fills a collapsed volcanic crater. In wet years, the lake is a robust crescent-shaped body of water that dominates the surrounding crater. In drier times, it is a sad marshy mud hole.

If you are lucky enough to visit when the lake is full, there will be plenty of opportunity to reach open water where various water-loving creatures congregate. You're likely to see grebes paddling across the water, mule deer bedding in the lake shore greenery, or prehistoric looking tiger salamanders darting beneath your boat. There is a healthy insect population along the shoreline, but the clouds of little buggers diminishes once out on the water.

Escaping the noise of the nearby forest roads is not so easy. Sounds carry in odd patterns around this circular crater. At times you will be able to hear a conversation from across the lake, while a slight wind shift will mask even the rumble of a nearby ATV.

Logistics: Take exit #306—the Stoneman Lake Exit—off I-17. This is about 34 miles south of Flagstaff, and 20 miles north of Camp Verde. It is about 6 miles of pavement before the road turns to dirt. Here you will make a left on road #213, and go another couple miles to road #213A, which leads to the lake. At the bottom of the hill, there is a road to the right that leads to a parking area and gravel launch ramp. The route is well signed.

High Country Lakes 91

Cruising the shoreline at Stoneman Lake

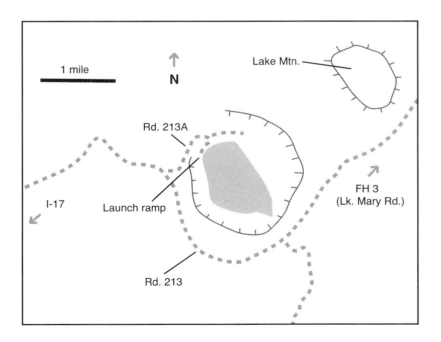

Blue Ridge Reservoir

General Description: A narrow reservoir in the pines of the Mogollon Rim
Motorized Traffic: Low / 8 hp max
Surface Area When Full: 292 acres
Shoreline When Full: 15 miles
Fish Species: rainbow trout
Elevation: 6,700'
Best Season: May — October

Blue Ridge Reservoir is an impoundment on the upper reaches of East Clear Creek. The dam creating the reservoir was built in 1963 by Phelps Dodge in order to secure water for an agreement with the Salt River Project.

Water was actually pumped out of Blue Ridge, and sent over the Mogollon Rim to the East Verde River where it ran downstream to the Verde River and Horseshoe Reservoir—an SRP lake. This additional water in the Salt system was in exchange for water that Phelps Dodge took out of the watershed near their mines at Morenci.

Whatever the political framework behind the lake might be, Blue Ridge is a pleasant mountain waterway with two main arms leading to forested canyons. Outcrops of Kaibab Limestone add to the scenery. A few minutes of paddling away from the small launch ramp will usually have you in uncrowded forest surroundings. With the extensive shoreline, the lake is especially conducive to overnight camping trips from the water.

Logistics: Take Highway 87 north from Payson, or south from Winslow, and turn east onto road #751 near milepost 295. It is 4 miles down this dirt road to a parking area and launch ramp on the reservoir. Another mile down the progressively rockier road will lead to the dam. There are no launch locations here at the dam.

High Country Lakes 93

A tandem canoe party explores Blue Ridge.

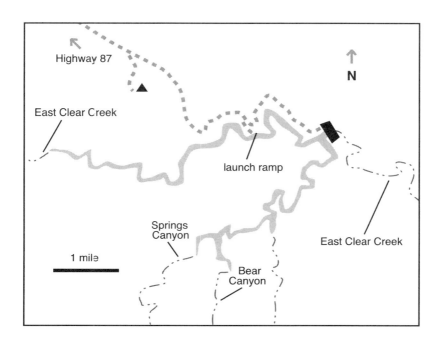

Knoll Lake

General Description: A clear water reservoir in the high country
Motorized Traffic: Low / electric motors only
Surface Area When Full: 60 acres
Shoreline When Full: 3.2 miles
Fish Species: rainbow trout
Elevation: 7,300'
Best Season: June — September

Many miles of dirt roads must be traveled in order to reach this waterway, keeping Knoll Lake off the radar of most weekend visitors. The relative remoteness of the area suits certain types of wildlife. On my visit here, I spotted bear tracks at both ends of the lake.

The lake is formed by an earthen dam on Leonard Canyon, a tributary of East Clear Creek. Leonard Canyon is also the boundary between the Coconino National Forest to the west, and the Apache-Sitgreaves National Forest to the east.

There are two arms to the lake, and a dome island which is responsible for the lake's name. The water here is inviting and clear, and the south-facing forest is open and stately, reminiscent of California's Sierra Nevada.

Logistics: Take Highway 260 east from Payson about 30 miles and turn left onto road #300. Follow road #300 (a.k.a. Crook Trail, Rim Road) for 20.6 miles and turn right onto road #295. (Road #300 is paved for the first 3 miles, then it is usually a dusty washboard dirt road. You will have to veer left onto #300 at the road #34 junction 9.5 miles from the highway.) Follow #295 for 4.5 miles to Knoll Lake.

High Country Lakes 95

Approaching the knoll of Knoll Lake

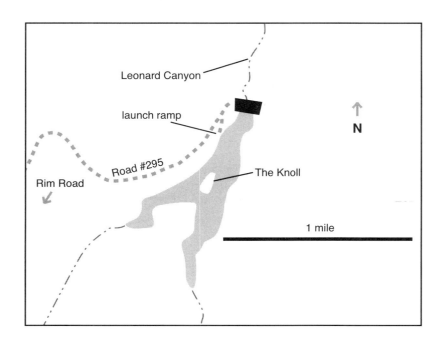

Woods Canyon Lake

General Description: A popular high country destination
Motorized Traffic: Low / 8 hp maximum, but plenty of small trolling motors use this lake.
Surface Area When Full: 70 acres
Shoreline When Full: 3.5 miles
Fish Species: rainbow trout
Elevation: 7,500'
Best Season: May — October

Woods Canyon Lake is no secret. This recreational reservoir near Highway 260 has served as refuge from the heat of the lowlands since it was created in 1955. A virtual metropolis of developed campgrounds lines the road on the approach to the lake, and there is a store located at the launch ramp.

Despite the popularity of this place, a quaint park-like atmosphere exists. Families line the banks as they cast for trout, and the lake waters are plied by aluminum rental boats, canoes, kayaks, and float tubes. All seem to be in search of the same thing, a relaxing day in the cool high country.

As usual, a little paddling beyond the central launch area will reward you with more elbow room, and sometimes even solitude. The lake waters snake back into three arms of upper Woods Canyon, which is the headwaters of the Chevelon Creek drainage. The three major lake arms each lead into luxuriant forest surroundings where meadows of clover and bracken fern sit beneath Douglas firs, Southwestern white pines, and of course the ubiquitous ponderosa pines.

The beauty of the place seems to have a palliative effect on its visitors, and a quiet calm usually reigns in the lake's upper arms. Woods Canyon Lake provides Arizonans with a peaceful high country experience, even if it isn't a secret.

Logistics: Take Highway 260 east from Payson about 30 miles and turn northwest onto forest road #300. This turn is 0.3 miles east of mp 282. There are signs for Woods Canyon Lake here. Take road #300 for 3.4 miles to road #105 (again, follow the signs), and follow this north for 1.5 miles to the lake.

High Country Lakes 97

A summer weekend at Woods Canyon

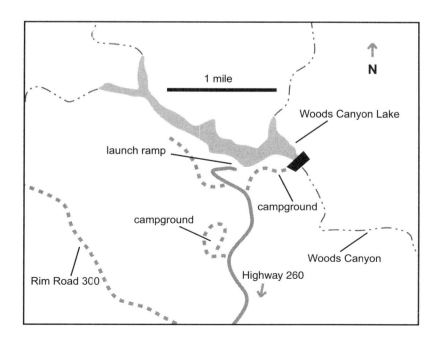

Willow Springs Lake

General Description: An open mountain lake on the Mogollon Rim
Motorized Traffic: Low to Moderate / 8 hp max, but I saw bigger motors here, and there is a dock accommodating mid-sized boats.
Surface Area When Full: 160 acres
Shoreline When Full: 5.3 miles
Fish Species: rainbow trout, largemouth bass
Elevation: 7,500'
Best Season: May — October

Willow Springs Lake is an easily accessible body of water near the crest of the Mogollon Rim. A paved road leads to waters edge, and a campground is adjacent to the lake.

Like Woods Canyon Lake just a few miles to the west, Willow Springs Lake is a popular high country destination. Unlike the forest-cradled feel of Woods Canyon, however, Willow Springs possesses an open expanse of water where visitors can actually get more than a couple hundred yards from shore. Both Woods Canyon and Willow Springs Lakes are impoundments on the headwaters of Chevelon Creek.

Logistics: Turn north off Highway 260 near mp 283 onto road #149. This is less than a mile east of the turn for Woods Canyon Lake. There is a sign for Willow Springs Lake. A paved road leads a mile from the highway to the water.

High Country Lakes 99

The open waters of Willow Springs Lake

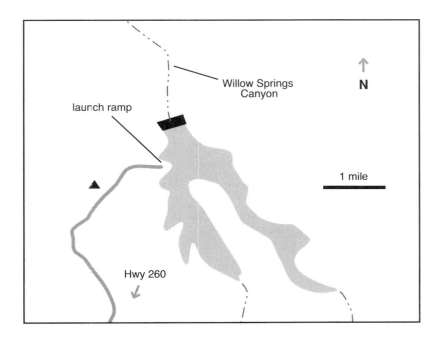

Prescott Pine-Tree Lakes

General Description: Two small lakes in the pine trees near Prescott
Motorized Traffic: Low / electric motors only
Surface Area When Full: Lynx: 60 acres Goldwater: 30 acres
Shoreline When Full: Lynx: 1.8 miles Goldwater: 1 mile
Fish Species: Lynx: rainbow trout, largemouth bass, channel catfish, sunfish, crappie Goldwater: largemouth bass, channel catfish, sunfish, crappie
Elevation: Lynx: 5,529' Goldwater: 5,990'
Best Season: April — November

Lynx Lake is located east of Prescott in a pine and chaparral covered basin below Spruce Mountain. The lake is an impoundment on Lynx Creek, one of the primary headwater sources of the Agua Fria River. It is a generally open lake, and bald eagles can be seen. The northwest shoreline is sometimes off limits to human traffic so the eagles can nest undisturbed. Boat rentals are available on the north shore. In 2007, prices were $12.50/hour or $35.00/day.

Goldwater Lake is smaller than Lynx, but like Lynx, it is located in a pine forest near Prescott. Tiny Bannon Creek is the source water for Goldwater. Below Goldwater is Lower Goldwater Lake, a city reservoir that is not accessible for recreation. Water from here continues downstream to Granite Creek, and then on to the Verde River. Boat rentals are available here for $10/hour. Both Goldwater and Lynx Lakes charge a $2 parking fee.

Logistics: For Lynx Lake, take Highway 69 east out of Prescott toward Prescott Valley. Just past the Prescott Gateway Mall, take Walker Road south for about 3 miles to the south shore access. There is a store and cafe on the north shore, but the south shore is the only place to launch boats.

For Goldwater Lake, take Mt. Vernon Avenue/Senator Highway south from Prescott about 3 miles to Goldwater Lake Road. It is about a half mile from here downhill to the lake.

High Country Lakes **101**

Canoeing in the pines

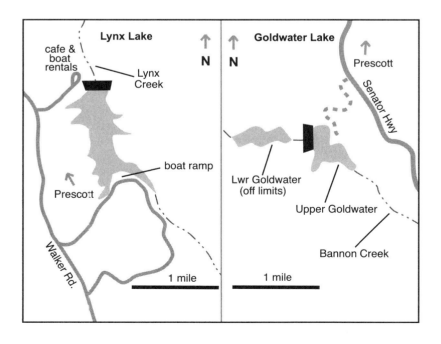

Prescott Granite Lakes

General Description: Two recreational reservoirs on the outskirts of Prescott
Motorized Traffic: Low / Watson—no motor restrictions, but no-wake rule is in effect / Willow—electric motors only
Surface Area When Full: Watson: 200 acres / Willow: 342 acres
Shoreline When Full: Watson: 5 miles / Willow: 6 miles
Fish Species: largemouth bass, crappie, sunfish, channel catfish
Elevation: Watson: 5,162' / Willow: 5,140'
Best Season: February — November

Watson Lake is the crown jewel of Prescott area lakes. Granite boulders weave maze-like throughout most of the lake, forming numerous coves to explore. If open water paddling is more your thing, the south end of the lake can be broad and windswept. Dead snags lean out of the water in this southern end of the lake, attracting cormorants and bald eagles. No swimming is allowed in the lake. Boat rentals are available for $10/hour.

Willow Lake is an impoundment on Willow Creek. Willow Lake fills a broad shallow basin, so during times of high water the lake expands dramatically. Due to the shallowness, algae and grasses are prolific throughout much of the waterway. Traffic is generally lighter here than at any of the other Prescott lakes. No boat rentals are available, swimming is not allowed.

Logistics: For Watson Lake, take Highway 89 north from Prescott a couple miles to a roundabout intersection for Watson Lake Park. Go right here and follow signs to the boat ramp and lake.

Willow Lake is north of Prescott off Willow Creek Road. Continue past the car dealerships and turn east on Heritage Park Road, which is located opposite Embry Riddle Aeronautical University. After turning off Willow Creek Road, take an immediate right and curve past ball fields to the lake access dock.

High Country Lakes **103**

Heading out to explore Prescott's Watson Lake

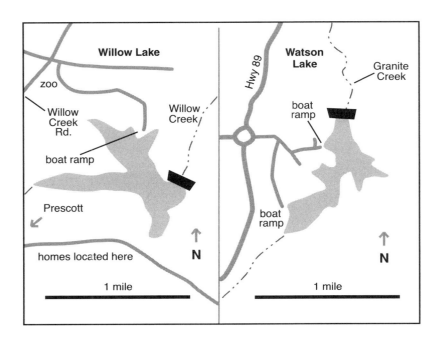

Fools Hollow Lake

General Description: A lake designed for recreation near the town of Show Low
Motorized Traffic: Low to Moderate (10 h.p. max)
Surface Area When Full: 150 acres
Shoreline When Full: 5.6 miles
Fish Species: brown trout, rainbow trout, largemouth bass, small mouth bass, crappie, sunfish, walleye, channel catfish
Elevation: 6,300'
Best Season: April — October

Paddling beneath cliffs at Fools Hollow

Located on the outskirts of Show Low, Fools Hollow Lake is fully developed for summer recreation. Several parking areas, picnic ramadas, and campgrounds encircle the water. Arizona State Parks administers the facilities, and a $6 fee is required to enter.

Once on the water, paddlers might want to view a wildlife habitat area near the southern tip of the lake. On the southeast arm of the lake there are lakeside residences, but the long northeast arm is more undeveloped. Low basalt cliffs border much of the shoreline, while ponderosa pines and junipers form the woodlands nearby.

Beneath the lake waters are the remnants of the Adair farm. Thomas Adair settled the bottom land along Show Low Creek in the late 1800s. Locals chirped that only a fool would try to farm the rocky substrate, prompting the name Fools Hollow.

Logistics: Turn off Highway 260 in west Show Low onto Old Linden Road near milepost 338. This turn is signed for Fools Hollow Lake. In about a half mile, turn left at the Fools Hollow Recreation sign, and proceed another 0.3 miles to the park entrance. There is a $6 fee to enter the park.

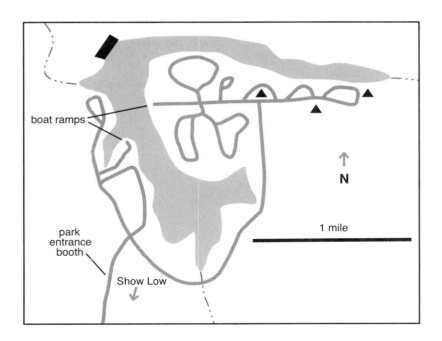

Rainbow Lake

General Description: An open waterway in the community of Pinetop / Lakeside, surrounded by homes
Motorized Traffic: Low
Surface Area When Full: 111 acres
Shoreline When Full: 3.5 miles
Fish Species: brown trout, rainbow trout, largemouth bass, sunfish, channel catfish
Elevation: 6,800'
Best Season: April — October

Rainbow Lake is surrounded by homes and private property. Using thoughtful foresight, the Game & Fish Department purchased public access to this water in the 1960s, prior to the extensive development that is there now. Please respect private property along the shoreline of this mountain retreat.

From the launch area on the north end of the lake, one can paddle southward across open water, or explore a few marshy areas near shore. Birdlife can be plentiful here. I saw herons, coots, eagles, and hundreds of ducks on my visit. Despite the wildlife, this is not a wilderness setting. The entire shoreline is decorated with houses, many of which sit vacant for most of the year. Lake paddlers can cruise the shoreline gawking and coveting the waterfront houses, or cast shame at the avarice, depending on one's world view.

Logistics: From Highway 260 in Pinetop / Lakeside, turn south onto Lakeview Lane. Lakeview Lane is located a quarter mile west of the Lakeside Ranger Station, or just west of the pond that is visible to the north of the highway.

High Country Lakes 107

A Wildcat fan paddles Rainbow Lake

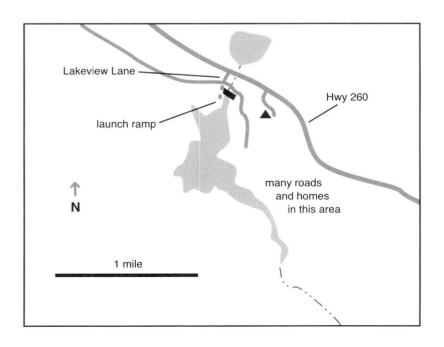

Lyman Lake

General Description: A reservoir and state park in northeastern Arizona
Motorized Traffic: Moderate / Personal watercraft and motorboats use the lake, but traffic is generally light.
Surface Area When Full: 1300 acres
Shoreline When Full: 16 miles
Fish Species: rainbow trout, largemouth bass, crappie, sunfish, channel catfish, walleye
Elevation: 6,000'
Best Season: May — October

There is a state park here with a store, boat docks, and a developed campground. In 2005, the entrance fee was $5 for one day. The launch areas near the park headquarters offer access to the water, but for small boats, there are less busy shoreline locales off a road that runs along the western shore of the lake.

The reservoir is big enough to develop some sizeable waves, especially here on the high plains where it is almost always windy. If you can make it across the choppy waters, there is an interesting pathway called "The Ultimate Petroglyph Trail." The trail is located just north of a limestone and shale outcrop on the eastern shore of the lake. There is an informational kiosk at the trailhead, and a path that leads uphill through a black basalt boulder field with some impressive petroglyphs.

Logistics: Lyman Lake is located off Highway 180/191 about 17 miles north of Springerville. There are signs leading to Lyman Lake State Park.

High Country Lakes 109

Petroglyphs at Lyman Lake

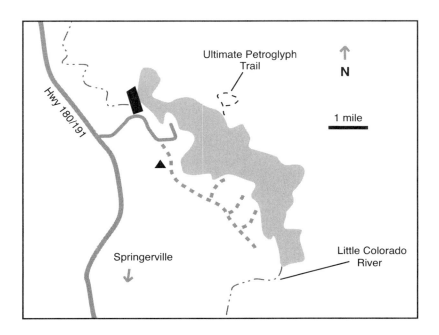

Carnero Lake

General Description: A small pond/lake in the White Mountains
Motorized Traffic: Low / single electric motors only
Surface Area When Full: 67 acres
Shoreline When Full: 1.5 miles
Fish Species: rainbow trout
Elevation: 9,000'
Best Season: May — October

This is a lovely mountain lake set on the northern edge of the White Mountains. Because of its 9,000 foot elevation, there is usually sufficient snowpack to recharge the lake every spring, providing areas of open water and marsh lands.

The marshy areas on the lake provide excellent habitat for bird life. Cattle sometimes graze nearby, and elk frequent the area. The sounds at Carnero Lake are often a cacophony of cow bellows, elk bugles, and bird song.

It can be a busy place of forest creatures, but Carnero Lake is rarely overrun by humans. This is a small, usually quiet lake on the fringe of Arizona's high country.

Logistics: From Springerville, take Highway 260 west about 9 miles, and turn north onto forest road #118 at milepost 385. Follow road #118 for 7 miles, and turn left onto road #117A. Three miles down #117A, make a left to Carnero Lake. It is about 0.5 miles from this last turn to the water.

High Country Lakes 111

Carnero Lake is on the cool northern edge of the White Mountains.

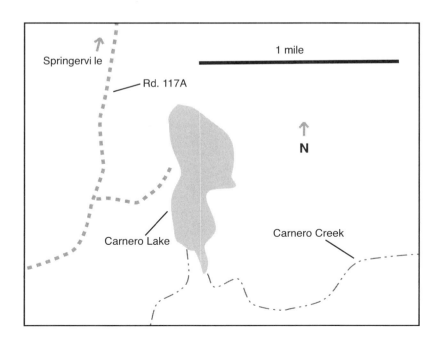

Greer Lakes

General Description: A trio of lakes near the mountain community of Greer
Motorized Traffic: Low / River Reservoir is open to 10 hp motors, while Tunnel and Bunch are electric motors only.
Surface Area When Full: Tunnel 43 acres / River 140 acres / Bunch 64 acres
Shoreline When Full: Tunnel 1 mile / River 2.8 miles / Bunch 1.6 miles
Fish Species: brown trout, rainbow trout
Elevation: 8,200
Best Season: May — October

There are three reservoirs here: Tunnel, River, and Bunch. All three are filled by the Little Colorado River just downstream of the mountain town of Greer.

Depending on irrigation needs, water levels between the three lakes can fluctuate dramatically. Following normal to wet winters, River Reservoir is full and overflowing down an impressive spillway, while at other times it can be almost dry, and only Bunch Reservoir will be releasing water downstream. Late in the year following irrigation season, these lakes are generally low.

Whatever the condition of the various ponds, there is usually ample water here for recreation. In summer, the lakes are popular with fishermen, but because there are three different waterways, no single reservoir gets too crowded.

Logistics: Turn south off Highway 260 onto Route 373 towards Greer. In 3.4 miles, turn left onto road #87B to the Greer Lakes. There are signs leading to all three reservoirs. The roads are paved.

High Country Lakes 113

Getting a workout at Greer Lakes

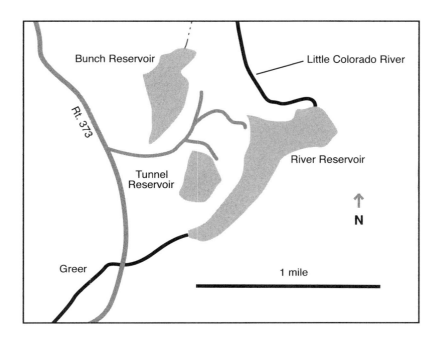

Big Lake

General Description: A large popular lake in the White Mountains
Motorized Traffic: Moderate / 8 hp maximum, but there are lots of small motors on the lake
Surface Area When Full: 439 acres
Shoreline When Full: 5.7 miles
Fish Species: rainbow trout, brook trout, cuttthroat trout
Elevation: 9,000'
Best Season: June — September

This is a classic Arizona summer destination. While desert cities melt under 100-degree heat, the breezy open waters of Big Lake are a comfortable or even chilly environment in mid-July.

Naturally, this high-country escape attracts outdoor enthusiasts throughout the summer months. There is a cadre of development to accommodate the high visitor load, including docks, campgrounds, a store, and boat rentals. Fortunately, the lake lives up to its name, and is big enough to accommodate a large number of users.

The two main launch areas are at the south end of the lake, and at the marina near the eastern shore. For kayaks and canoes, there are also other places along the lakeside road where a short carry will have you at the water.

Logistics: The easiest approach to Big Lake is via Route 261. This road heads south off of Highway 260 just west of Springerville. It is about 20 miles on the paved Route 261 to Big Lake. The route is signed all the way.

High Country Lakes 115

Big Lake below Mt. Baldy

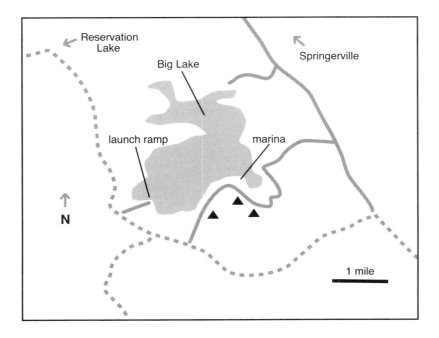

Luna Lake

General Description: A small lake near the town of Alpine
Motorized Traffic: Low / 8 hp maximum
Surface Area When Full: 120 acres
Shoreline When Full: 3 miles
Fish Species: rainbow trout, cutthroat trout
Elevation: 7,900'
Best Season: May — October

This is a local's lake near the quaint mountain town of Alpine. The lake is formed by a dam on the San Francisco River. Below Luna Lake, this river flows into nearby New Mexico before coming back into Arizona and joining the Gila River near Clifton. Here at the river's headwaters, Luna Lake provides paddling opportunities with good wildlife watching potential.

One of only two pair of breeding bald eagles in the White Mountains resides along the shores of Luna Lake. The great birds can often be seen swooping over the water to snatch unsuspecting fish for a quick meal. Paddlers will also notice buoys near the west end of the lake. These indicate the boundary of an area reserved for waterfowl only, free from human interference.

Logistics: From Alpine, take Highway 180 toward Luna, New Mexico for about 4 miles. There are signs for Luna Lake, located on the north side of the highway.

High Country Lakes 117

Luna Lake near Alpine

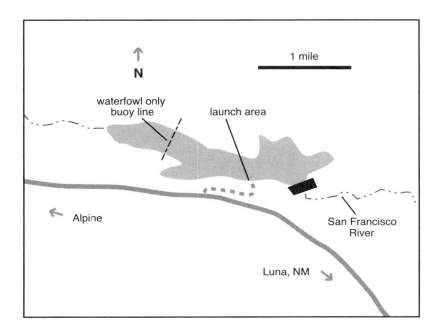

Reservation Lake

General Description: A medium-sized lake in lush forest on the Apache Reservation
Motorized Traffic: Low / no gas engines, but plenty of small electric motor trolling boats
Surface Area When Full: 293 acres
Shoreline When Full: 5.5 miles
Fish Species: brown trout, rainbow trout, brook trout
Elevation: 9,000'
Best Season: June — September

This is an impoundment on Reservation Creek, a beautiful mountain stream draining the southeastern slopes of Mt. Baldy. This sacred mountain is clearly visible from the lake, and the general scenery of the area is wonderful.

Reservation Lake's 9,000 foot elevation, and its location on the southern flanks of Mt. Baldy means that it gets the full brunt of the wettest winter storms, and summer monsoons. This moist locale produces the most dense forests in the state. The life zone is officially known as the Canadian Zone, and certain views in the area could indeed be mistaken for Canada. Englemann spruce is the dominant tree here, but there is also a diverse mix of blue spruce, aspen, Douglas fir, corkbark fir, Southwestern white pine, and ponderosa pine. This green canopy lines the shores of Reservation Lake—a deep clear reservoir in Arizona's "little Canada."

Remember that a valid reservation permit is required to boat here.

Logistics: Take Highway 260 east from Pinetop for 24 miles to Route 273. Follow 273 (it starts paved, then turns to dirt) past the Lee Valley Recreation Area, and turn right onto road #116 at the edge of the Big Lake Recreation Area. This is about 15 miles from the highway. Follow road #116 about another 11 miles to Reservation Lake. The route is signed well.

High Country Lakes 119

Morning glass at Reservation Lake

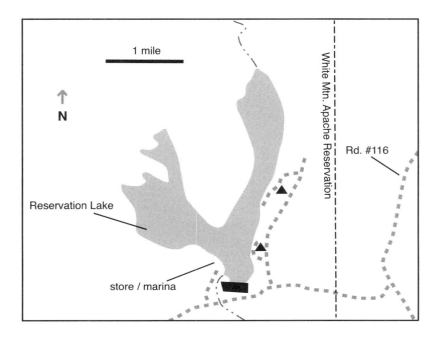

Parker Canyon Lake

General Description: A recreational reservoir in the foothills of the Huachuca Mountains
Motorized Traffic: Low
Surface Area When Full: 129 acres
Shoreline When Full: 3.6 miles
Fish Species: brown trout, rainbow trout
Elevation: 5,400'
Best Season: April — October

This is a relatively deep, clear lake formed by an earthen dam on a modest creek. It is a favorite weekend destination for fishermen out of Sierra Vista, which is located just over the mountains from Parker Canyon Lake. There is a campground overlooking the lake, and a small community of homes on the mountainside nearby.

Parker Canyon is located on the remote western slope of the Huachuca Mountains. Here the terrain drains into the upper Santa Cruz River, which trickles through a broad grassland valley as it flows south into Mexico. Then the river makes a U-turn. Heading north now, it re-enters the United States near Nogales, and runs onward through Tucson.

Logistics: Take AZ Route 83 south from Sonoita, AZ for about 30 miles. Follow the signs for Parker Canyon Lake.

High Country Lakes 121

Parker Canyon Lake in southern Arizona

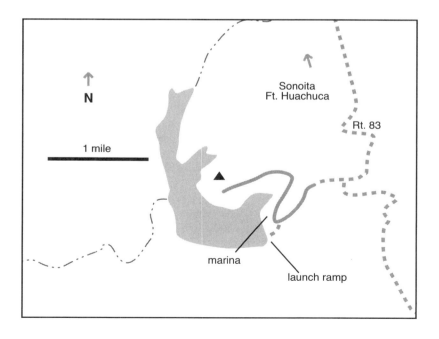

WHITEWATER RIVERS

Whitewater Rivers

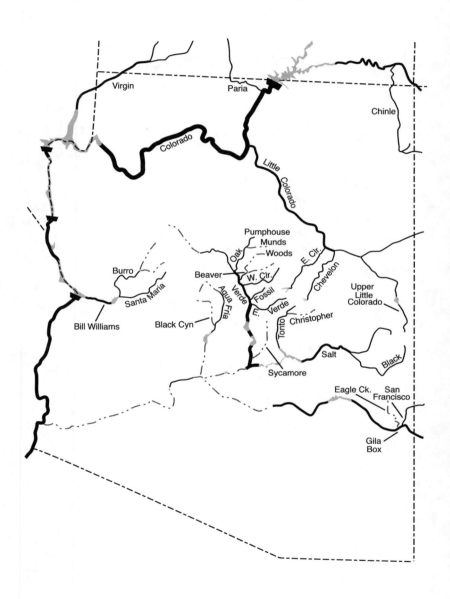

Arizona River Running Seasons

The river running season in Arizona is an elusive and erratic beast. In drier than normal years, there is no season at all. The Mogollon Rim forests gather only a meager winter snowpack, and the desert remains dusty throughout all seasons. In wet years, however, several feet of snow accumulates in the high country, and the low deserts become a verdant landscape of green grass and mossy springs. Arizona is a land of extremes, and only about a third of the time does this region experience a happy medium of precipitation.

Pacific storms can begin to move through Arizona as early as **October**. These autumn cold fronts sometimes combine with subtropical hurricane remnants, and the combination of weather systems can produce colossal rains, bringing rivers up throughout the state. **November** occasionally ushers in a series of storms producing both rain and snow, and thus high water. More often than not, however, fall is a time of blue skies, and it is not unusual for the Mogollon Rim to be snowless into **December**. This is the time when the Arizona snowpack really gets a chance to start accumulating, as short days and a low sun angle minimize evaporation and melting.

Mid-winter often produces the biggest floods in Arizona. These events result from low pressure systems which draw copious subtropical moisture up from the south. When the resulting heavy rain falls on an established snowpack, big water results.

February is the month when Arizona paddlers start to pay attention. The Sonoran Desert is often sufficiently saturated by this point in the winter to produce runnable streamflows with each passing storm. At higher elevations, February is a crucial period. Warm sunny weather at this time can result in a dreaded "trickle off," in which the runoff begins too early, bringing rivers up slightly, but not high enough for good paddling. If February is cold and snowy, however, things are setting up perfectly for a good **March**—the time of year when Arizona streams are most likely to be running.

Spring often arrives quickly at this latitude, with a few days of high atmospheric pressure bringing mountain temperatures into the 50s or 60s, resulting in a rapidly melting snowpack. These warm spells are sometimes followed by big snowstorms that can extend the paddling season into April. If unsettled weather persists, **April** can be a prime paddling time in Arizona, but things are drying out fast. The only river in Arizona likely to running by **May** is the Salt, which drains the 11,000-foot-high White Mountains. The Salt can continue with elevated flows into **June**, but this is rare. The entire state is usually dry and hot by summer solstice.

But wait, **July** means the monsoon season is arriving, and hope is rekindled in the Arizona paddler's psyche. As subtropical moisture invades from the south, heavy thunderstorms often result, producing brief periods of high water. "Brief" is the operative word here. Paddlers might consider using weather radar to predict runnable flows during monsoon season, as rivers are often already dropping when "real-time" flow data is available over the internet. The monsoon comes in a random cycle defined by bursts and breaks. During a burst, clouds, humidity, and widespread rain are dominant, making Arizona feel like an exotic tropical paddling destination. Before planning an **August** paddling safari for Arizona, however, remember that monsoon thunderstorms are usually scattered, and it takes a significant downpour to generate runoff. Whitewater junkies are well-advised to stay in British Columbia during late summer. The monsoon retreats to Mexico by mid-**September** most years, and it is time again to pray for next winter's storms.

Arizona Hydrology

Paddling rivers in Arizona requires close attention to the weather, and a commitment to be ready to put in at a moment's notice. The reason for this mandatory fireman-like readiness? Water fluctuation.

Arizona has the most dynamic hydrology in the United States. Arizona rivers that normally carry a measly base flow of 200 cfs can spike to over 100,000 cfs, and normally dry riverbeds can suddenly flood at 50,000 cfs or more. These high water events rarely last long, however. A river in the eastern United States, for example, might rise to a peak level and gradually return to a base flow over the course of a few days, whereas an Arizona river can peak and fall over the course of a few hours.

Even when Arizona streams are running from snowmelt (rather than rainfall), the daily fluctuation between the afternoon melt and the nighttime freeze is greater than in other regions. It is not unusual for a snowmelt-fed Arizona creek to fluctuate from a morning low of 300 cfs to an evening high of 1,000 cfs, thus changing the stream's character dramatically over the course of a single day. "Riding the wave" of runoff is more than just a theoretical euphemism in Arizona. It is the truth. So get your boat loaded and ready, it's time to go boatin'!

Before gluing yourself to the internet flow page waiting for that magical river level, perhaps we should discuss Arizona hydrology as it relates to paddling.

One important factor in Arizona streamflow is the snow level. As you might have guessed, the snow level is the elevation above which precipitation falls as snow, and below which precipitation falls as rain. Snow levels usually drop over the course of a storm, falling with the passage of the associated cold front. A very cold storm in Arizona will have a snow level of 4,000 feet or less. In these instances, paddlers should not expect exceptionally high water, as the precipitation on river headwaters will be frozen into the form of snow. A warm winter storm will bring snow levels of 8,000 feet or higher. Assuming there is some snowpack on the ground, a storm of this nature spells flood.

The ideal snow levels for Arizona paddlers are 6,000 to 6,500 feet. Environments below these elevations are too warm to maintain a snowpack, so any snow that falls at these low elevations is quickly lost to evaporation and low intensity runoff. When the snow level is over 6,500 feet, only the highest headwaters gain a snowpack. Drainage basins between 6,000 and 6,500 feet that might otherwise collect snow are quickly flooded away by rainfall, and a potentially long spring season is replaced with a short-lived winter flood.

Soil and rock substrates also affect streamflows. Unfortunately, Arizona's highest mountains (the 12,000-foot-high San Francisco Peaks) are made of porous cinders, and very little surface runoff is gained from these sometimes snowy mountains. The nearby western Mogollon Plateau is slightly better for producing runoff. But this too is a porous crack-filled geologic landscape of basalt and limestone. On the other end of the substrate spectrum are the slickrock deserts of Northeastern Arizona. Here much of the land is solid rock, and most of the moisture that falls runs off immediately. Central Arizona's granitic soils are perhaps the best for producing runoff yet also slowly releasing water in the form of springs and seeps.

Of course all of this information is disseminated by the professionals at the National Weather Service and the United States Geological Survey, and much of that information is readily available to the public.

Water Year Graph

As indicated in the previous summary of Arizona boating seasons, mid-February to mid-April is generally the paddling season in Arizona. However, flows are erratic, and can occur at any time of year. Additionally, different streams run at different times. Therefore, a formula was devised to produce the following graph, which depicts the length of a given paddling season over the past 40 + water years (Water years begin October 1st, and end September 30th.).

Using hydrologic records, I selected four geographically varied creeks (Santa Maria, Oak, Tonto, Chevelon), and counted the number of days per year each stream was high enough to paddle. I also counted the number of days per year the Salt River was over 500 cfs (roughly a minimum rafting level), as well as the number of days it was over 1,000 cfs (a "good" level). In order for a particular date to be counted as a "season day," two or more creeks had to be running. Days in which only one of the selected creeks was running counted as half a season day. When no creeks were running, but the Salt was over 1,000 cfs, I recorded one third of a season day. If no creeks were running, and the Salt was only over 500 cfs, I recorded one fourth of a season day.

If you follow any of this, your mind is as convoluted as mine, and I suggest you seek professional help. For the rest of you who stopped reading at the top of the page, here is the gist of it: The below graph roughly represents the length of whitewater paddling seasons in Arizona over the past four decades.

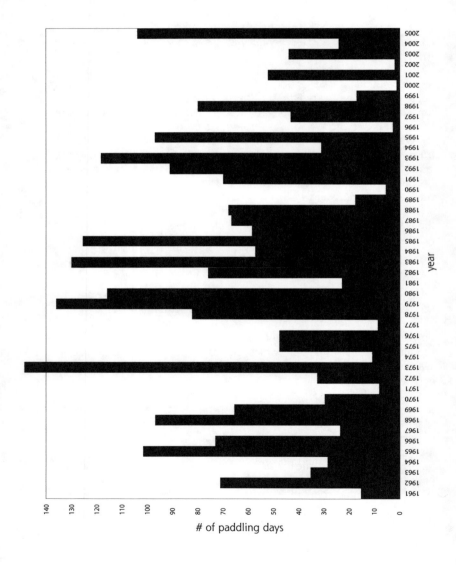

How to use this book—Whitewater

There are two types of whitewater descriptions in this book: standard listings with accompanying maps, and secondary runs described only with text. Standard runs are the rivers that run in a normal water year, and have relatively easy access. Secondary runs are the more obscure and esoteric rivers and creeks that don't get paddled very often. In the case of Grand Canyon and the Virgin River, they are well documented elsewhere, so a full description here would have been redundant. These popular rivers are listed as secondary runs.

All whitewater river descriptions are arranged geographically, roughly from north to south. The secondary runs are squeezed in the pages between the standard runs of a given region. The book is arranged this way to offer convenient information for visiting paddlers who might be looking for an alternative to the standard rivers. Below is a guide to the category listings for the standard streams.

General Description: This is a brief basic overview of the river segment.

Difficulty: This is the class rating of the river based on the international scale of whitewater difficulty. The ratings given here are based on the general character of the run as a whole at recommended water levels. When one or two outstanding rapids on a particular run are more difficult than the rest, this is indicated by a second classification numeral given within parenthesis. For example, III (IV) means that the run is generally class III, but there is a rapid or two on the run that is class IV. A plus + or minus - symbol (IV+, V-) further defines the specific difficulty rating.

Gradient: This is the vertical drop, in feet per mile, of the river segment. The overall gradient of the run is listed first, followed by a mile by mile gradient when important.

Length: The total distance of the described run.

Flow: There are two flows listed here: Minimum and Ideal. The minimum flow is what I consider to be a practical minimum for the run in a hard shell kayak. Many of these rivers can be run at lower levels than this book's listed minimums, especially when using inflatable kayaks. For hard boats, however, I think you will find my minimum levels rather bony, and a good cut-off guideline. A minimum flow for rafts is generally the low end of the ideal range. Ideal flows are, again, based on my interpretation of what is optimal. Maximum flows are not listed in this book, because how high you are willing to run a river is a judgment only you can make. Any water level greater than the ideal range should be considered high water. Of course Arizona rivers fluctuate greatly, so it is always a guessing game as to what the actual level is at the time when you put-in. Launching on any river is always, ultimately, a product of your own judgment.

Gage: Listed here are the USGS gages that are most useful for the particular river. I have listed the name of the gage as it appears on the Real Time AZ Streamflows website: http://waterdata.usgs.gov/az/nwis/current/?type=flow

Shuttle: The shuttle distance required for the described run. Also listed are road surfaces, and whether or not the shuttle is a good candidate for hitchhiking or bicycling.

Elevation: The elevations of the put-in and take-out for the run.

Likely Season: This is the time of year when a given river is most likely to have runnable streamflows. For more on Arizona paddling seasons, consult "Arizona Boating Seasons" in the introduction.

Peak Flow: The highest water level ever recorded for the stream, and the date on which that occurred.

Whitewater Rating Scale

Below is the whitewater rating scale as listed by American Whitewater—the leading whitewater paddling organization in North America. If you run rivers, you should be a member of AW. Check them out at **www.americanwhitewater.org**.

This is the American version of a rating system used to compare river difficulty throughout the world. This system is not exact; rivers do not always fit easily into one category, and regional or individual interpretations may cause misunderstandings. River difficulty may change each year due to fluctuations in water level, downed trees, recent floods, geological disturbances, or bad weather. Stay alert for unexpected problems!

As river difficulty increases, the danger to swimming paddlers becomes more severe. As rapids become longer and more continuous, the challenge increases. There is a difference between running an occasional class IV rapid and dealing with an entire river of this category. Allow an extra margin of safety between skills and river ratings when the water is cold or if the river is remote and inaccessible.

Class I Rapids
Fast moving water with riffles and small waves. Few obstructions, all obvious and easily missed with little training. Risk to swimmers is slight; self-rescue is easy.

Class II Rapids: Novice
Straightforward rapids with wide, clear channels which are evident without scouting. Occasional maneuvering may be required, but rocks and medium-sized waves are easily missed by trained paddlers. Swimmers are seldom injured and group assistance, while helpful, is seldom needed.

Rapids that are at the upper end of this difficulty range are designated "Class II+".

Class III: Intermediate
Rapids with moderate, irregular waves which may be difficult to avoid and which can swamp an open canoe. Complex maneuvers in fast current and good boat control in tight passages or around ledges are often required; large waves or strainers may be present but are easily avoided. Strong eddies and powerful current effects can be found, particularly on large-volume rivers. Scouting is advisable for inexperienced parties. Injuries while swimming are rare; self-rescue is usually easy but group assistance may be required to avoid long swims. Rapids that are at the lower or upper end of this difficulty range are designated "Class III-" or "Class III+" respectively.

Class IV: Advanced
Intense, powerful but predictable rapids requiring precise boat handling in turbulent water. Depending on the character of the river, it may feature large, unavoidable waves and holes or constricted passages demanding fast maneuvers under pressure. A fast, reliable eddy turn may be needed to initiate maneuvers, scout rapids, or rest. Rapids may require "must" moves above dangerous hazards. Scouting may be necessary the first time down. Risk of injury to swimmers is moderate to high, and water conditions may make self-rescue difficult. Group assistance for rescue is often essential but requires practiced skills. A strong eskimo roll is highly recommended. Rapids that are at the lower or upper end of this difficulty range are designated "Class IV-" or "Class IV+" respectively.

Class V: Expert
Extremely long, obstructed, or very violent rapids which expose a paddler to added risk. Drops may contain large, unavoidable waves and holes or steep, congested chutes with complex, demanding routes. Rapids may continue for long distances between pools, demanding a high level of fitness. Eddies may be small, turbulent, or difficult to reach. At the high end of the scale, several of these factors may be combined. Scouting is recommended but may be difficult. Swims are dangerous, and rescue is often difficult even for experts. A very reliable eskimo roll, proper equipment, extensive experience, and practiced rescue skills are essential.

Class VI: Extreme and Exploratory Rapids
These runs have almost never been attempted and exemplify the extremes of difficulty, unpredictability and danger. The consequences of errors are severe and rescue may be impossible. For teams of experts only, at favorable water levels, after close personal inspection and taking all

precautions.

Surfing the Web and the Waves

National Streamflows: http://waterdata.usgs.gov/usa/nwis/rt
Arizona Streamflows: http://waterdata.usgs.gov/az/nwis/rt
Colorado Basin River Forecast Center: http://www.cbrfc.noaa.gov/

It is hard to believe that there was desert paddling before the internet, but there was. These were the days when paddlers had to employ the telephone ("How hard is it raining there? Is the creek clear or brown?"), their own hydrologic knowledge, and intuition. I remember when the first internet real-time flow data was introduced to me. It seemed too good to be true. The availability of internet-provided flow information has certainly increased the feasibility of paddling in Arizona, and aided in the exploration of new rivers here. The drive to explore, however, is as old as mankind, and Arizona rivers have seen adventurers since long before "internet" was even a word.

Arizona River Running History

It is likely that river running in Arizona began as soon as humans inhabited the Southwest. Although river travel was not integral to ancient Arizona cultures, the Mogollon, Sinagua, and Salado people probably used simple boats on rivers in the area.

Documented river runs of the first Europeans in Arizona are elusive, although there are vague reports of mountain men floating through the countryside on occasion. River running, however, was never a major source of exploration here. That all changed in 1869.

That is the year John Wesley Powell and his crew ran the Colorado River through Grand Canyon. With their trip, they filled a great blank on the maps of the day, and set a standard for river exploration that can never be equaled. The Powell party traveled mostly unknown territory, negotiating class IV and even V whitewater en-route. Their run through Grand Canyon remains the greatest first descent of all time, and it took place right here in Arizona.

Except for subsequent river trips on the Colorado, nearly a century went by before river running got a solid stroke in on other Arizona rivers.

The Salt River began seeing descents in the 1950s, with the Theodore Roosevelt Council of Boy Scouts generally recognized as the first to run the river. Pete Weinel of the Tonto National Forest, and Dr. John Ricker were the leading authorities on the Salt throughout the 60s, running the river in rafts at a multitude of water levels.

In the 1970s and early 80s, several factors coalesced, creating ripe conditions for river exploration. Environmental awareness was on the increase, plastic kayaks burst onto the scene replacing the fragile fiberglass of old, and the weather cooperated, providing nearly a decade of consistently wet winters from 1978 to 1985. It was the golden age of paddling in Arizona.

A center of paddling activity during the period was Prescott College, an alternative institution that drew adventurers to Arizona from across the country. One of these adventurers was Brad Dimock.

Dimock bought a kayak directly from the father of plastic kayak manufacturing—Hollowform inventor Tom Johnson. The year was 1973. The boat cost $129.95. Dimock learned slalom technique from nationally renowned racer Chuck Stanley, then returned to Arizona and found himself part of a gang of enthusiastic dirt-bag river-guide paddlers who were always up for hair-brained adventures.

Dimock and his cohorts made several notable Arizona first descents including Chinle Creek, Chevelon Canyon, the Paria River, and most significantly, the Little Colorado River Gorge. Dimock reflects, "Throughout all the adventures there were several things that never changed. The equipment was minimal, the vehicles marginal, the food adequate at best."

In 1979, two of Dimock's paddling partners, Wayne Van Voorhies and Kim Reynolds, took whitewater exploration up a notch with their descent of the Agua Fria River. The duo launched in Dewey, Arizona, and emerged at the I-17 in Back Canyon City three days later.

Other adventuresome boaters were knocking off the obvious runs by the early eighties. Joe Sharber and Jeff Bowman were probably the first to paddle Oak Creek on a cold snowy day in March, 1981. In eastern Arizona, the Metzger brothers, Kirk and Kris, were exploring the upper Little Colorado and upper Black Rivers, while paddler Steve Williams was pioneering upper Salt River tributaries.

During the late winter of 1983, a large group set off on the unknown East Verde. After two days of occasional wipeouts and frozen fingers, the majority of the party took out at Doll Baby Ranch to go catch a Joni Mitchell concert. Glenn Rink decided to stay with the river, and pressed on by himself. He became the first to run the entire East Verde, and probably the last to run it solo.

This bold and independent approach to river running exhibited by Rink was also a trademark of Dugald Bremner—perhaps Arizona's most renowned paddler. Another Prescott College product, Bremner was a natural paddler, and had a thirst for adventure. Always one to keep quiet about his latest backcountry haunt, it is difficult to ascertain what exactly Bremner ran, or when. It is likely, however, that he was the first to run lower West Clear Creek, lower Tonto Creek, upper Oak Creek, and the Salt River's Flying V Gorge, all between 1979 and 1985. Dugald was still investigating new runs over a decade later as he and Allen Haden went steep creeking on Pumphouse Wash and Rattlesnake Canyon. Dugald and I pushed our limits on a first descent of Munds Canyon in 1997. Tragically, Dugald drowned on California's Silver Fork of the American less than two months after our Munds descent. If he were he still with us, Dugald would surely still be at the forefront of Arizona river exploration today.

Like the early '80s, the early 1990s brought a series of wet winters, and Arizona paddling continued to grow. Eagle Creek was paddled by Van Voorhies, Rink, and Bryan Brown in 1992. The off–limits Cibecue Creek is rumored to have been run by Brown and a Colorado contingent the following year. Also in 1993, Pat Phillips and Eric Seifer made the first push into Sycamore Creek's Butterfly Canyon, and lower Sycamore Creek was run by a group of Phoenix-area paddlers led by Jim McComb and Rob Reiterman. Four years later, McComb and Reiterman notched the most significant new Arizona run in over a decade with their descent of Tonto Creek's Hellsgate Canyon.

Well-timed spring storms produced an exceptional paddling season in 1998, presenting the opportunity for paddling on several new runs including Burro Creek, the Santa Maria River, upper West Clear Creek, and Woods Canyon. Prolonged drought suppressed river exploration for the next several years, but the wet winter of 2004-2005 again saw paddlers searching out new runs. McComb pushed farther upstream on Tonto Creek, leading a group down the headwaters above Hellsgate. Aaron Riding initiated the first runs of Black Canyon north of Phoenix, Fossil Creek was run on high water just prior to its base flow being restored, and a trio of Colorado paddlers (Evan Stafford, Todd Gillman, and Kyle McCutchen) completed the waterfall-riddled Christopher Creek Gorge. In recent years, Cody Howard has furthered Arizona paddling potential by exploring several low volume high gradient streambeds, including the Salome Creek Jug gorge, upper Salome Creek, Queen Creek above Superior, and his most significant descent, Poland Creek. Turkey Creek in the Bradshaw Mountains also saw its first descent in 2008. In that same year, Butterfly Canyon on Sycamore Creek finally saw a complete descent.

Despite its storied past, Arizona river exploration remains an ongoing quest. As this book goes to press, a few major whitewater streams in Arizona remain unrun, not to mention the many less obvious paddling destinations that magically spring forth with every good storm cycle. May your shuttle road be intact and the water level hold as the next ribbon of flowing water looms on the horizon!

Back when throwing ends meant something...

...and creek boating was yet a developing realm

Little Colorado River
(LCR Gorge – Cameron to Grand Canyon)

General Description: A Southwestern classic
Difficulty: IV
Gradient: 24 fpm/steepest mile is 70 fpm
Length: 59 miles
Flow: Minimum: 600 cfs
　　　　Ideal: 1,000 — 2,000 cfs
Gage: Little Colorado near Cameron. You'll also want to note the flows on the LCR at Winslow, Moenkopi Wash, and the Puerco near Chambers to estimate what water is potentially on the way. Make sure there is an adequate flow in Cameron before setting out. Lots of Little Colorado water disappears into the sand between Winslow and Cameron. Once making it to Blue Spring 12 miles above the confluence of the Colorado, there is a base flow of 200 cfs.
Shuttle: About 60 miles if you hike out the Powell Route, with navigation and guesswork necessary. About 160 miles if you continue through Grand Canyon to Diamond Creek.
Elevation: 4,100'—2,700'
Likely Season: March, April, August, September
Peak Flow: Estimated 120,000 cfs, September 20, 1923

Most boaters know the Little Colorado simply as a scenic attraction along the banks of the main Colorado River in Grand Canyon. The "Little C" (as locals call it) is normally an idyllic paradise in its lower reaches, tumbling over travertine ledges and swirling into deep turquoise-blue swimming holes. Following snowmelt or widespread rain, however, the LCR turns into a thriving pungent river of red.

Runnable flows here are erratic. Although the Little Colorado drains a significant portion of the southwestern United States, it is often just a sandy wash. The headwaters of the Little Colorado are found in the 11,000-foot high White Mountains of eastern Arizona. Spruce-lined mountain brooks at the source would seemingly provide a year-round flow to the arid lowlands, but these mountain streams get swallowed by irrigation and desert sands before ever reaching the lower gorge. Creeks emanating from the nearby 8,000-foot Mogollon Rim are the main source of water for the LCR in springtime, when an average or above average snowmelt produces runnable water levels in the gorge.

The first complete descent of the Little Colorado Gorge was made in 1978 by Grand Canyon boatmen Brad Dimock and Tim Cooper. The duo struggled against March cold in the shadowy depths of the canyon, stopping more than once to build warming fires. Once on the mighty Colorado, they raced down twenty-six familiar miles of river to Phantom Ranch, where a hike out of the Canyon would commence. Park rangers stepped in, however, arresting the pair for paddling the Colorado River in Grand Canyon without a permit. The adventurers were helicoptered directly to the Coconino County jail in Flagstaff to await trial for their heinous crime. Apparently, first descent glory sometimes comes with a price.

To avoid the first descenters' fate, refer to the logistics below to learn how to run the river legally. Once these logistical hurdles are passed, it's on to the river with fingers crossed that the water level holds!

Floating beneath the Highway 89 bridge at Cameron, paddlers will immediately notice the most striking feature of the Little Colorado: sediment load. The Little Colorado runs as muddy as they come, leaving a brown film on kayak decks, covering paddles with slippery clay, and coating skin with a layer of caked beige dirt. The novelty of paddling this river of mud quickly wears off when one realizes that the water is much too silty to drink (even after overnight settling), requiring all drinking water for the trip to be hauled in. Too much mud-water in the eyes has temporarily blinded paddlers here in the past, so keep the head-dunking to a minimum.

The first several miles below Cameron is a wide riverbed, providing an easy desert float. As jointed cliffs of buff-colored Kaibab Limestone emerge, the canyon quickly matures from a shallow draw to a narrow, even claustrophobic gorge. The sandy white Coconino formation forms the narrowest passage, as vertical walls squeeze the river into a cleft only twenty feet wide.

Fortunately, there are no rapids in this narrow spot. They begin below a tourist overlook 15 river miles downstream from Cameron. Rockslides that have terminated in the river form the first of several class IV boulder gardens on the run. If these first drops prove too intimidating, there are two escape routes from the gorge near the overlook. Unless you are comfortable with heights, however, the escape routes might be more

Running travertine ledges on the Little C

intimidating than the rapids.

The canyon is 1,000 feet deep and growing at this point. Soon you will be descending through the upper layers of Grand Canyon's geology—Hermit Shale, Supai formation, and Redwall Limestone.

The Redwall ushers in a new type of rapid different from the boulder sieves upstream. Travertine dams begin to span the river in multi-tiered drops. The travertine is most prolific below Blue Spring—a highly mineralized source that is responsible for the Little Colorado's turquoise color during low water. When flows get over 2,000 cfs, the travertine rapids go from class IV to class V, as large nasty hydraulics form.

The only named rapid—Atomizer Falls—provides excitement even at moderate levels. This folding chute tends to submerge paddlers in a dark brown froth. The action mellows to class II and III for the last few miles to the confluence, offering an opportunity to study the incredible towering landscape.

Logistics: There are two approaches to paddling the river legally. One is to join your permitted river trip at the confluence of the Colorado, and proceed through the remainder of Grand Canyon. If the stars are not in perfect alignment allowing this to happen, you can hike out of the gorge at the confluence of the Colorado via the Walter Powell Route. Boats have been carried out this route, but I don't recommend it. My advice would be to bring an old boat that you can do without for awhile, stash it in the rocks a mile above the confluence, and arrange for a river trip to pick it up and haul it out for you. Get a camping permit from the Navajos at the visitor center in Cameron before setting out.

The Walter Powell Route starts about 0.5 miles upstream from the confluence, near a 30-foot high arch on river right. For detailed directions to this route, refer to the book *Grand Canyon River Hikes*. Or you can just wing it like a trio of kayakers did in 2003. They forged a new route out of the canyon that involved free-soloing 5.7 faces with hundreds of feet of exposure. They survived. *Grand Canyon River Hikes* retails for $18.95.

To drive to the top of the Walter Powell Route, take the main dirt road off highway 89 at Cedar Ridge. Follow this reservation thoroughfare (RD. 6110) west, then veer southwest on progressively smaller roads. By the time you reach the rim of the canyon you will be on a two-track in the sagebrush. Expect several wrong turns. Be polite to any Navajos you might bump into out there, and they might be able to steer you in the right direction. With a copy of the river hikes book, a map, some patience, and a GPS, you will eventually find the top of the route.

The put-in is at the old highway bridge in Cameron.

Whitewater Rivers 139

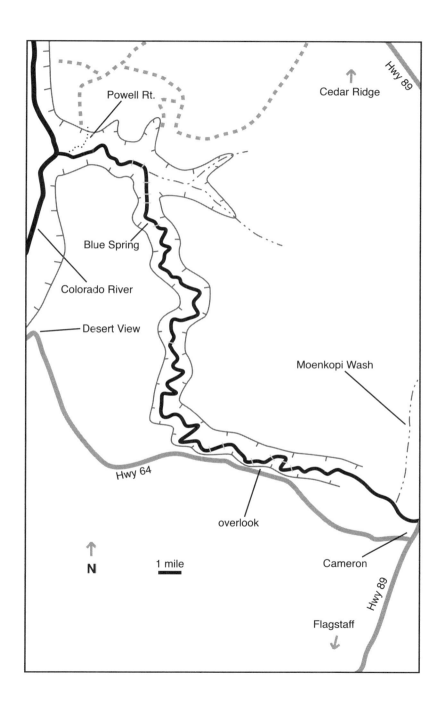

Chinle Creek

Chinle Creek drains the Chuska Mountains in northeastern Arizona via Canyon de Chelly. Portions of this sandy wash in the canyon have been paddled, but obtaining permits from the tribe and/or park service for the activity would likely be difficult, and it is a very visible place.

Below Canyon de Chelly, Chinle Creek runs out into the desert and often sinks into the sand or gets used up by people. One spring when Chinle Creek was cranking from snowmelt, my wife, Lisa, and I planned to put-in 50 miles downstream of Canyon de Chelly at the Highway 160 bridge. We arrived to find about 0.25 cfs in the creek. Ever since that disappointing non put-in, we refer to the nearby Navajo village of Many Farms as TOO Many Farms.

If you want to catch lower Chinle Creek below Highway 160, you will have to go when both upper Chinle and Lukachukai Creeks are running. Even then, Chinle Creek is little more than a muddy ditch. About 100 cfs keeps the ditch deep enough to paddle on, and the channel appears to be able to handle about 1,000 cfs before spreading into the flood plain.

Keep in mind that it is 40+ miles to the San Juan River from the highway, so you'd better have enough runoff to last three or four days. You'd be well advised to let the creek run a couple days before putting on, too, so that it has a chance to saturate the sandy river bottom and actually make it to the San Juan. An optimal level is probably 300 to 500 cfs. With this much water there are a few runnable waterfalls that whitewater junkies will love, although most of the time these 10-to 50-foot waterfalls are portaged. Whitewater is not the main attraction on Chinle. You should only come here if you are into desert scenery and indian ruins. Both are spectacular.

Paddling through Comb Ridge

Paria River

The Paria is a classic desert hiking route through a long winding canyon of Navajo Sandstone. It is a huge drainage, and occasionally has enough water to paddle on.

In the first version of this book, I reported that Brad Dimock and Wayne Van Voorhies were responsible for the first descent, in the early '80s. Theirs was almost certainly the first hard-boat run, but I've since learned that Utah boater Pete Chatelain ran the Paria as early as 1979. His two-man party used 10' rafts with oars, and took two days for the run. That first trip was such a success that they returned for another run a few years later. The Chatelain duo were also early boaters on the Escalante River to the north.

I ran the Paria solo in a day and a half during February of 1993. The entire run is forty-something miles long.

The first few miles below Highway 89 are ridiculously meandering as the swollen stream rumbles beneath crumbling cutbanks. Just as you get used to the scenic desert float, the canyon quickly forms, and a nerve-wracking unforgettable sluice through the Paria narrows begins.

At the level the river was when I ran it (300—500 cfs?), it wasn't too fast or deep to prevent me from slowing down if I had come upon a river-wide strainer. This might not be the case with higher water, however. The walls are smooth and vertical, making the slot rather committing and unscoutable. Enjoy the ride, because barring disaster, you'll soon be spit out into a broader canyon where Buckskin Gulch comes in.

Below here the river is less constricted, and regains typical river characteristics like eddies and riffles and waves. There are gravel bars to get out on, and you can float peacefully and gaze up at the awesome desert scenery. I encountered one logjam, which was easily portaged.

The next whitewater comes when the Moenave formation hits the river. A series of class II and III rapids ushers you out of the canyon and into the more open debris-filled valley that leads to Lees Ferry.

When the terrain opens into this final broad canyon, the whitewater picks up. Numerous rockslides terminate in the stream, forming pool-drop boulder gardens. The rocks are sharp and it takes relatively high water to make many of the rapids runnable. Dimock and Van Voorhies were foiled by big boats and low water on their run. The walking was so frequent, they eventually stopped putting on their sprayskirts between portages. I recall running a few of these drops, then camping with nightfall. When I woke the next morning, the water level was lower (down from 500 cfs to 100 cfs?), and everything was sieved out, so I too began paddling between drops without my sprayskirt. The portage fest didn't last long, however, and even with low water there was still enough to float out past bewildered cattle to the Lees Ferry bridge.

Oak Creek
(Indian Gardens run)

General Description: A lively roadside creek with wood
Difficulty: IV
Gradient: 75 fpm
Length: 5 miles
Flow: minimum: 200 cfs
ideal: 400 — 600 cfs
Gage: Oak Creek near Sedona
Shuttle: 4.6 miles, hitchable
Elevation: 4,600'—4,200'
Likely Season: March, April
Peak Flow: Sedona gage—23,200 cfs February 19, 1993.

This is the local creek for paddlers who live in Flagstaff and Sedona. The easy access and simple shuttle makes it ideal as an after-work run for those who can sneak away from their desks a few minutes early! The creek can get cluttered with logs, so all drops should be approached with extra caution. Paddling Oak Creek when the water is rising (and wood is moving) can get scary in a hurry. Because of the plentiful strainers, Oak Creek never quite attains "classic" status. Nevertheless, weaving through the boulder gardens on Oak Creek beneath towering cliffs of red rock is Arizona paddling at its finest.

The put-in at Indian Gardens is located just downstream from the confluence of Munds Canyon, which usually doubles the flow of Oak Creek. Interactions with curious tourists (and sometimes locals too) are common at this high-profile put-in. Garland's Store across the highway has cold beverages, and good deli food.

The creek splits in the first few hundred yards below Indian Gardens before reuniting into a swift channel that leads into the first rapid. This is a short, steep drop that contains a large hole at the entrance during higher flows. A couple more boulder bar rapids lead to the Trout Farm bridge. At lower flows, you can limbo under the left side of the bridge, otherwise, you must portage. Be quick about it, respect private property on river left, and stay out of the way of traffic!

Trout Farm Rapid, below the bridge, is generally a bony affair. At the bottom is a long pool that leads to Compound Fracture—a drop on a sharp right turn against a rock wall. This rapid often collects strainers, so proceed with caution. Below Compound, there is a short ledge sometimes called Reverse Compound, and a screaming-left-turn rapid that leads to a mellower section of creek before things begin to heat up again above Grasshopper Point.

Casner Canyon sometimes adds significant water to the creek about a quarter-mile above the next major rapid—a two-part cataract listed on the

Whitewater Rivers 143

Dampman on Oak Creek

following map as Supai Surf. Here the creek splits, forming a broad gravel bar on the right, and a narrow tree-lined channel on the left. Just below is the second part of the rapid, a steep boulder drop.

Pick Your Poison is next. This is a forested gravel bar that rarely has a clean line and is sometimes an obvious portage. In the pool below this nasty rapid you are likely to see others enjoying the creek, as the Grasshopper Point parking area is on river right. Just around the corner is Grasshopper Falls. The 5-foot vertical drop is the biggest boof on the run.

The surroundings get more spectacular as Highway 89A climbs high above the river gorge. Small side creeks pour in from river left, and the dramatic walls of the canyon burst with color in afternoon light. This scenic section is laced with several nice drops leading down to Midgley Bridge, a bedrock rapid that is the highlight of the trip. The sluice is rife with surf waves, and a hole at the entrance sometimes provides more entertainment than desired.

Just below Midgley there is a hole that can get sticky at certain levels. Once past this, the meat of the run is behind you. As you enter the town of Sedona, beware of a couple rapids that collect wood. The final rapid above the bridge provides a final bit of surf potential as the creek runs over slabs of red Schnebly Hill Sandstone. Taking out amidst new age energy and red rock majesty puts a perfect finishing touch on this gem of Arizona paddling.

Logistics: The take-out is in Sedona at the Highway 179 bridge. The put-in is along Highway 89A at Indian Gardens. This is 4.6 miles from the 179 bridge, and 1.8 miles north of the entrance to Grasshopper Point. If the creek looks too low at the Indian Gardens put-in, you can sometimes salvage the day by putting in at Grasshopper Point. The channel on this part of the creek is runnable at lower levels than up above.

Whitewater Rivers 145

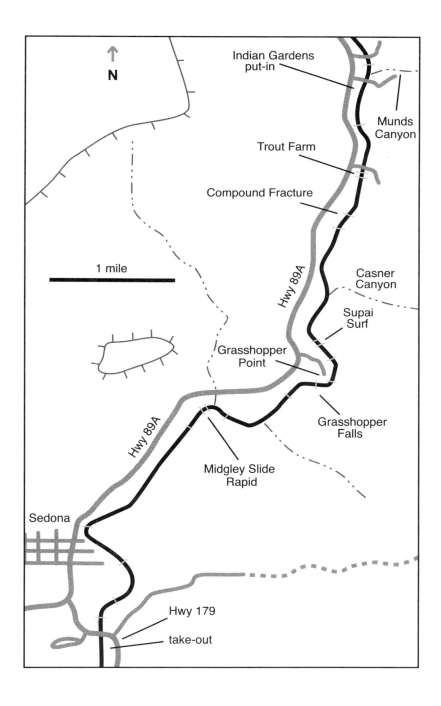

Little Colorado
(Grand Falls run)

When the Little Colorado is running high (over 2,000 cfs), Grand Falls is quite a spectacle. Even parking on the nearby canyon rim leaves you in a fine mist of mud emanating from the impressive roaring falls. The experience of putting in below this natural wonder is worth the effort regardless of the downstream run.

The biggest rapids on this run are at the take-out and the put-in. If you are not interested in whitewater (actually its brown water here), you can launch below the class III rapid which runs alongside the crude put-in trail. It is not a long carry to the water, but it can be muddy, slick, sharp, and steep—not a recommended place for rafts.

Once leaving the grandeur of the Grand Falls put-in, you'll be floating a wide desert river between modest sandstone cliffs. There are pictographs on the canyon walls that a keen eye will likely spot. A few class II rapids punctuate the run, but mostly this is a scenic float. Although it has been run at 1,000 cfs, I recommend higher water levels, as the riverbed is very wide and shallow in places. I have run this stretch at 2,000 cfs, and prefer even more.

If you do catch the Little C at a booming high flow, don't fall asleep above Black Falls! This is a river wide basalt ledge/diversion that forms a symmetrical terminal hydraulic. The take-out is immediately below here, reached via a road heading northeast out of Wupatki National Monument.

Oak Creek
(upper reaches)

Above the confluence of Munds Canyon (the standard Indian Gardens put-in), the flow in Oak Creek usually diminishes by half, leaving the upper creek too low for paddling. It is difficult to know when upper Oak Creek will have a good flow, as a multitude of tributaries throughout the canyon contribute different amounts of water at different times. As a very general rule, good levels for upper Oak Creek occur when Oak Creek at Sedona is running 800 to 1,500 cfs, or sometimes lower when the water is coming from the upper reaches of the watershed. When there is adequate water in the upper creek, some of Oak Creek's best whitewater can be found here.

The two-mile section from Manzanita Campground to Indian Gardens contains good class III+ to IV- whitewater, but strainers tend to collect in this stretch even more than in the rest of the creek. Most years it is a woody portage fest, and I avoid it. There are also two bridges on this part of the creek that are quite dangerous to paddlers.

Because of these hazards, it is often best to take out at Manzanita Campground after running the most excellent Slide Rock section upstream. Banjo Bill or Halfway Campgrounds can both serve as put-ins for this run.

There is nice tight class III—IV creeking through basalt boulders in the first part of the Slide Rock Run. Halfway Rapid (just below the Halfway parking area) is the first notable drop as a crumbly cliff juts into the river from the left. Not far below here, the creek races through a gauntlet of trees and boulders before entering a red rock gorge above Slide Rock. The entrance rapid—Chunky Monkey—is class IV+, or V at some levels. It features a complex entry above a "chunky" boulder bar that finishes on a left-to-right flume. It can be easily portaged. There is some nice surfing as the river zooms through the gorge down to Slide Rock Rapid. This is a great class IV bedrock slide that gets big (but usually remains flushy) at higher water. Lower Slide Rock is the standout rapid on the run, usually a class V-. Below here the creek goes under the highway and hides in a small canyon. Side creeks pour in as waterfalls, and pool-drop class III and IV boulder rapids are the rule. Watch out for strainers as you approach Manzanita Campground.

Upstream of the Slide Rock Run, above Banjo Bill Campground, there are several good drops and the steepest gradient (140 fpm) on the creek. A parking area across from Don Hoel's Cabins can serve as a put-in. Excellent eddie-hop water starts things off, building to the crux of the section at an S-turn rapid coined by Flag boaters Bill Morse and Eric Brown after a desperately bad pop song called "Boom Boom in the Zoom Zoom." If you make it through the boom boom, you'll be zooming through the zoom zoom. Several paddlers, including yours truly, have swum here. A rapid just above Junipine Resort is the next highlight—long and technical, often with spicy wood hazards. Don't swim here, because just downstream there is a grate bridge behind Junipine Resort that is a serious hazard. A quarter-mile below, a rapid just above Banjo Bill Campground serves as a rockin' finish to the section. This part of the creek is great fun when the level (250—400 cfs, visual) is good. Don't be fooled by the inviting glimpses of the river from the road. At high water, this section gets out of control quickly.

Upstream from Don Hoel's cabins, there are scenic slow pools intermingled with fun class III—IV rapids. Above the West Fork of Oak Creek there is one junky rapid at a road crossing that you can see from the highway, and several stretches of river that are more oak than creek. A few fun drops linger, however, within a small riverbed of primarily class III tree-laced whitewater. Upstream from the bridge at the bottom of the switch backs is Pumphouse Wash. See that description for details.

Oak Creek
(Sedona - Red Rock Crossing)

General Description: A scenic and tree-infested run in Sedona
Difficulty: III
Gradient: 48 fpm
Length: 5 miles
Flow: minimum: 300 cfs
      ideal: 600 — 800 cfs
Gage: Oak Creek at Sedona.
Shuttle: 11 miles, bikeable, mostly paved.
Elevation: 4,200'—3,900'
Likely Season: February, March, April
Peak Flow: Cornville gage—26,400 cfs February 19, 1980. Sedona gage—23,200 cfs February 19, 1993.

This is a class II—III run, but due to plentiful tree hazards it is only advisable for solid class III boaters or better. Most of the spookiest rapids are narrow alleyways between walls of alders. Dealing with encroaching branches is a requisite skill for this run, and don't be surprised if you have to make a last minute micro-eddy or tree grab to avoid a strainer.

That said, this is a totally worthwhile run with decent play and great scenery. I have had many enjoyable days on this stretch. Sandstone ledges are sprinkled throughout the run, providing good surf potential, especially at higher levels. Class IV or better paddlers will enjoy this run when it is 1,000 or even 2,000 cfs. Less skilled boaters should steer clear of Oak Creek when it is this high, however, as the strainers can come fast.

There are two standout rapids. The first comes about 0.5 miles below Chavez Crossing—a low water road crossing that forms a river-wide ledge. Screaming Right is created by several large blocks of sandstone that have fallen into the creek from a river left cliff. As you might guess, the move is a ferry to the right. The other notable rapid, Turtle Island, is also formed by a big chunk of red rock. At high water, Turtle Island becomes a large hole occupying the middle two thirds of the river. At more moderate levels, it splits the current into narrow channels on either side.

When you see tourists lining the river right bank taking your picture, you'll know you're nearing the take-out at Red Rock Crossing. There are a series of ledges here that serve up some nice surfing at the right levels (generally medium-high). To top it all off, the backdrop for this surf zone is a picture-perfect formation called Cathedral Rock.

Logistics: The put-in is located at the Highway 179 bridge in Sedona, right at the gage. There are take-outs on both sides of the river. The river right take-out is within Red Rock State Park, so a fee is charged. To find the river left take-out from the put-in, take Highway 179 about six miles to the

Whitewater Rivers 149

Paddling Oak Creek after a channel-cleansing flood

Village of Oak Creek, and turn right on Verde Valley School Road. Take this road about five miles to a parking area located a couple hundred yards from the creek, and road's end.

Surfing into the postcard

Will Viktora jumpin' in—Winery Waves on lower Oak Creek

Whitewater Rivers 151

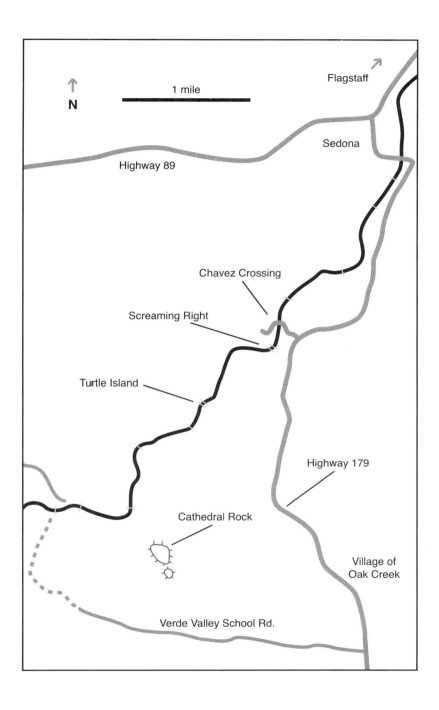

Pumphouse Wash

Pumphouse Wash is the main headwater stream of Oak Creek, south of Flagstaff. It is a dramatic canyon incised in Coconino Sandstone, and cloaked in maple, fir, and pine.

When Oak Creek is running big from snowmelt (over 1,000 cfs), Pumphouse often has a runnable window. Flows in Pumphouse range from under 100 cfs at the put-in to 500 cfs or more at the take-out. When it has enough water to paddle, Pumphouse is usually on the rise from afternoon snowmelt, making it an especially challenging undertaking. There is plenty of wood, the top gradient on the creek is over 200 fpm, and the canyon is vertical and committing. If all this sounds like your idea of a good time, read on.

The first descent of Pumphouse occurred in 1995 by Dugald Bremner and Allen Haden. They had big excitement when Allen got stuck in a hole and Dugald came barreling down right behind him. Bremner used his compadre's upside down boat to skip over the hydraulic and make an eddy. Allen continued with his mostly-inverted-one-man-rodeo until finally swimming out and making his own eddy. They recovered all the pieces, and finished the run without further mishap. The boat-skipping rapid is one of the standouts, featuring a tricky twisting entrance leading to a ten-foot drop, and a powerful hole. Immediately below is a boulder strewn rapid that ends in sheer walled narrows.

The second descent of Pumphouse was a solo mission I undertook after unsuccessfully driving Oak Creek Canyon looking for a partner. Things went well until a bedrock slide rapid where I learned that sandstone has a bit more friction than say, polished granite. My bow came to a screeching halt on the "slide." I spun sideways and dropped into a walled-in hole, where an overhanging tree prevented me from rolling up. Seeing that my roll attempts were futile, I pulled my skirt and was quickly flushed to the sandy bottom, and downstream. My kayak tumbled in the hole while I got my wits together, and then it dutifully drifted staight to me! The rest of the run went fine, but I was glad to make it out on a rapidly rising 600 cfs.

In 2004, Harlan Taney and I ran a 15-foot basalt falls near the put-in, and everything went smoothly until daylight began to wane in the narrow gorge. Our race to beat darkness made for a rushed pace, which made for a few terrifyingly out-of-control runs. We gleefully floated under the highway with a good 45 seconds of light to spare. There have been several descents of Pumphouse since. Although it is a more relaxing run when daylight's aplenty and the water level is stable, a run here is nearly always a full-on adventure. There is one rapid in the canyon that is essentially a must-run pinched between vertical walls. A portage here would take over an hour and some rope work. There is also a river-wide log that has been stuck in a narrow spot for many years. It can be portaged at river level, but it is a nerve-wracking ordeal.

Pulling into camp on Apache Lake

Paddling Blue Ridge

Topock Gorge on the Colorado River

Touring on Lake Powell

High Country paddling

Peña Blanca Lake hides in the Atascosa Mountains

Canoeing on Watson Lake near Prescott

Gila River below Kelvin

The San Francisco River beneath the Mogollon Mountains

Spring paddling on Oak Creek

Chiapas or Arizona?

Roy Lippman shreds it on Burro Creek

Rail Slide—Agua Fria River

Probing Pumphouse

Boofing in the saguaros

The new Quartzite Falls at 9,000 cfs

The take-out is the Highway 89A bridge. The put-in is downhill from the junction of roads #237 and 89A, about 1.5 miles north of the Oak Creek Overlook. Traveling the canyon on foot at low water is a great hike (see *Canyoneering Arizona*). Being there during high water is an unforgettable experience.

Munds Canyon

Dugald Bremner drew my attention to Munds Canyon as a potential kayak run in the mid-1990s. I hiked the dry creekbed soon after, and paddling Munds soon became a top priority for us. Following a four day snowstorm in early April of 1997, we got out the maps and started to get excited. The gradient read 130, 240, 300, 360, 280, 280, 220, and the steepest section pushed over 400 fpm. It was steeper than anything either of us had run, but our confidence was soaring with the seemingly limitless potential of our new creekboats. I recall pleading to my older, wiser, and more skillful companion, "We can do it. We've got Freefalls."

With bright spring sunshine turning a blanket of snow into sheets of water, we set out. By the time we checked the creek level at the put-in, drove our shuttle, and got back to launch along I-17, it was 11 a.m. The hour was late for a first descent, but the water was just arriving as the day warmed, so an earlier put in would have been fruitless anyway.

We launched on 100 cfs and scraped and bounced our way down the little creek. About a mile into the run, the gradient picked up, making the water seem higher. Soon after this, side creeks began pouring in, and the water *was* higher. We ran a beautiful 75-foot basalt slide and were really finding our rhythm just as the water began to spike, and we entered the narrow and steep Coconino Sandstone section of canyon.

Waterfalls were raging off the canyon rims, and the creek had turned from clear to a turbid, roaring brown. We were now on 500 cfs or more. Our existence became moment to moment—a nonstop blur of assessment, execution, and reaction. My notes from the trip bring back poignant memories: "Just as we entered the Coconino, we came to a spooky rapid with a horrible looking portage on the right. I ran down the left, finishing against a sheer cliff and banging my boat in a funky chute. I waited for Dugald to show. He was upstream, out of view, and isolated from me by vertical cliffs. If anything happened, I was helpless to assist. It was the longest minute of my life. Finally he came plunging through the gap. His paddle hit rock on both sides of the chute and went rebounding out of his grasp. He calmly hand-paddled into an eddy and snatched it out of the current as it drifted by. We were relieved and nervous, confident and scared—fully alive."

That is pretty much how it went for the next hour. I got stuck in a surging eddy for three cycles at one drop. Dugald was surfed in a hole for a minute at another. At yet another, we were both completely submerged and spit out like watermelon seeds.

We both beached tenuously and scrambled out of our boats above a blind slot narrows. As I began to assess the scout, Dugald commandingly said, "We should hike out now." I was too lost in the moment to realize that only an hour of daylight remained, and even a scout of the narrows below us would take 20 minutes.

The hike was epic. Thick chaparral, cranking side creeks with class V crossings, and of course, darkness. We made it to my truck and returned to Flagstaff where we rested and licked our wounds the entire next day.

By the following day the creek had dropped significantly. Dugald was busy with work, and not terribly psyched to paddle any more of Munds anyway. So, Eric Brown hiked back in with me and we bashed out of there on less than 100 cfs. I tried Munds one other time with Harlan Taney and Pat Phillips. We ran the first two miles and hiked our boats out of the canyon (not an unreasonable option at that point), back to the put-in.

If you decide to make a run on Munds, here is the strategy: Launch at midday or later to get maximum water for the first couple of miles. Study your topo map, stash your boats, and hike back to your car. River right has multiple routes out of the canyon, and once on top, it is an easy walk through meadows and open forest back to the freeway. The next day, get up early and hike back in. Paddle through the Coconino Sandstone (the steepest crux part of the canyon) on morning's low water, and then let the afternoon rise catch you for the last mile or two out to Oak Creek. There are a couple great slide rapids just before reaching Oak Creek, but watch out for wood in them. Good luck!

Munds Canyon

Pumphouse narrows

Beaver Creek

General Description: An easily accessible and pleasant float in the Verde Valley
Difficulty: II
Gradient: 20 fpm
Length: 8 miles
Flow: minimum: 150 cfs
       ideal: 300 — 700 cfs
Gage: Beaver Creek below Montezuma Well. You can also add the flows of Wet Beaver and Dry Beaver Creeks together. It's been my experience that adding the two flows is more accurate than relying on the Beaver Creek gage.
Shuttle: 5 miles, hitchable, bikeable
Elevation: 3,400'—3,200'
Likely Season: March, April
Peak Flow: 33,000 cfs (estimated) September 5, 1970

Beaver Creek is a convenient and worthwhile run for those who want a class II alternative to the Verde. The run actually starts on Dry Beaver Creek, which usually contributes 60 to 70% of the total flow for Beaver Creek during periods of high water. The rest of the water comes from Wet Beaver, a perennial stream popular for its summertime swimming holes.

Not far below the put-in, you will pass the confluence of Wet Beaver as the river bends beneath tall cliffs and begins a horseshoe bend away from the freeway. The creek maintains this winding course for the entire run, making for a longer river distance than you might expect given the relatively short shuttle.

The long sweeping bends of the creek will usher you past overhanging walls and awesome sycamore trees. You might even spot a beaver sliding down the muddy banks. We did.

The most challenging rapids are created by trees in the channel. One root ball in particular could have ugly consequences for the unwary paddler. On the brighter side, there are a few surf waves to be found in the class II wave trains.

A small rapid rushes in front of Montezuma Castle. Drifting along beneath the green river banks and arching sycamore trees, it is easy to see why the Sinaguan people of days past picked Beaver Creek as their home.

Logistics: The take-out is at a road crossing adjacent to a narrow foot bridge over Beaver Creek along Middle Verde Road. This is about 1.5 miles from I-17, near Camp Verde High School. To reach the put-in, head north on I-17 for 3 miles to exit #293, and drive to the low water crossing of Dry Beaver Creek.

Whitewater Rivers 157

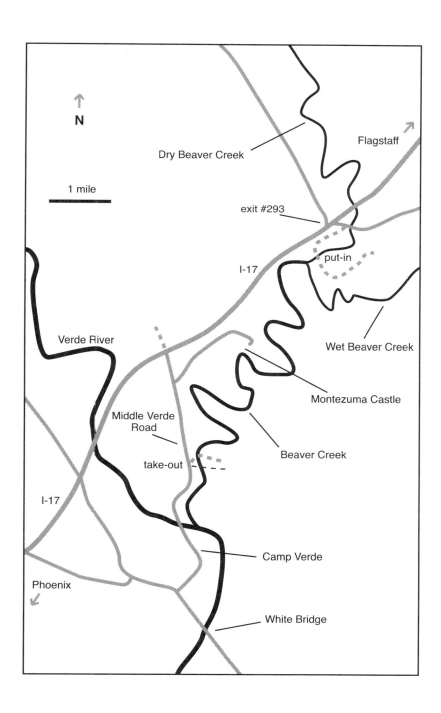

Oak Creek
(lower reaches)

Oak Creek below Red Rock Crossing contains several varied and worthwhile stretches. The gradient lessens as the creek leaves the Mogollon Rim and approaches the Verde River. Trees make the stream difficult to manage in some places, so paddlers who venture here should be accustomed to dealing with brush and strainers. Despite the abundant vegetation, I have had many pleasant days of paddling on these lesser-known sections of Oak Creek. Most of the lower runs are runnable down to 200 cfs, perhaps lower if you don't mind dragging from time to time. For class II-III paddlers, levels of 300 to 500 cfs are probably ideal. More experienced boaters will want slightly more water.

Red Rock Crossing to Red Rock State Park is class II-III, with plenty of brush and trees to avoid. My notes read "...full of trees. In a nutshell, pretty lame." Salvation can be found, however, in one nice Supai ledge early in the run that makes a fantastic play wave.

The creek from Red Rock State Park to Dry Creek provides pleasant scenery. After winding past homes in the first mile, the surroundings change to rolling hillsides of cactus and red rock. There are a couple constricted class II drops, and of course your standard Oak Creek rapids consisting of tree-studded gravel bars.

Dry Creek to Page Springs contains the best whitewater on lower Oak Creek. Here the creek cuts through basalt and conglomerate as it leads into a desert canyon. There are a few class III rapids, along with plentiful birdlife. At the take-out in Page Springs, there is a play hole that comes alive at levels over 700 cfs.

The Page Springs to Cornville stretch also contains several surf-friendly ledges, the best being a series of play waves located near a winery. The defining characteristics of this run, however, are the lush grottoes of vegetation on the banks, and the many mellow class I-II riffles.

If you are in search of mellow whitewater, nice scenery, or just a day spent on the water away from others, lower Oak Creek could be the river for you.

Dry Creek

Only in Arizona would a watercourse named Dry Creek be a paddling destination. Although most of the time this creekbed is in fact dry, during high water events it carries enough water to float. Dry Creek is often the best option in the area when standard runs like Oak Creek are so high that they are carrying trailers and bridges downstream.

Flood conditions in the region often make Dry Creek just about right for paddling. I have run it at 800 cfs (when Oak Creek was 15,000 cfs), and a meager 100 cfs (when Oak Creek was about 2,000 cfs). Both trips were pleasant and memorable.

There are two runs to pick from: The upper run starts where Dry Creek Road goes over (or maybe under) the creek just west of Sedona. An obvious take-out for this section is Highway 89A. It is a class II (III) run with a hitchable shuttle. The lower run is from 89A to Oak Creek. This is class III, featuring some awesome cypress trees on the banks and in the creek.

Dry Creek drains the spectacular Mogollon Rim country west of Sedona. Much of the water comes from this forested high country, but sand and sandstone along the creek's lower reaches make the water very gritty and sediment laden. Keep those eyes closed!

Matt Fahey preparing to launch on Dry Creek

Verde River
(White Bridge to Beasley)

General Description: A quiet stretch of river below the town of Camp Verde
Difficulty: I — II
Gradient: 10 fpm
Length: 9 miles
Flow: minimum: 150 cfs (many die-hards run it lower)
   ideal: 400 — 1,000 cfs
Gage: Verde near Camp Verde
Shuttle: 11.2 miles, bikeable
Elevation: 3,100' — 2,900'
Likely Season: Anytime the river is not exceedingly low
Peak Flow: Camp Verde gage—119,000 cfs February 20, 1993.

This section of the Verde serves as a great introduction to river running for beginners, and a relaxing float for more experienced boaters. There are a couple small rapids toward the end of the run, and plenty of tree obstacles that will test your skills, but the main attraction here is the peaceful riverine environment. Herons, kingfishers, and hawks are common along this stretch. Paddlers with a keen eye for wildlife might even spot the elusive river otters that play the currents on this part of the Verde.

Not far below the White Bridge, there are a couple of tree-lined channels of swift water, so first-time paddlers should get the basic strokes down before charging downstream too eagerly. The river bends to the left and drifts past some palatial riverside homes before curving south and into a more rural setting a couple miles into the run. Views of Squaw Peak and the Verde Rim dominate the southwestern skyline, while the Mogollon Rim rises to the east.

Just beyond halfway to the take-out, West Clear Creek enters on the left. The debris from the outflow of West Clear Creek forms a small riffle, the first in a series of rapids that come in the final miles above Beasley Flat. You will know you are nearing this take-out when the white cliffs of the geologic Verde formation become more distinct, and the river makes a right turn along their base. There are some ledges in here that make playful whitewater, with decent surf waves at higher flows. Beasley Flat is just below. Take out here unless you are ready for several miles of class III action that starts around the next corner.

Logistics: The take-out is at Beasley Flat. To get there, take Salt Mine Road off of Highway 260 in Camp Verde. It is 8.8 miles down Salt Mine Road until the road turns to dirt. Go left here, and continue 2.4 miles to the Beasley Flat river access area.

The put-in is located at the White Bridge over the river just south of Camp Verde. There is parking and river access on river left. This is a couple tenths of a mile from the Salt Mine Road/Highway 260 intersection.

Whitewater Rivers 161

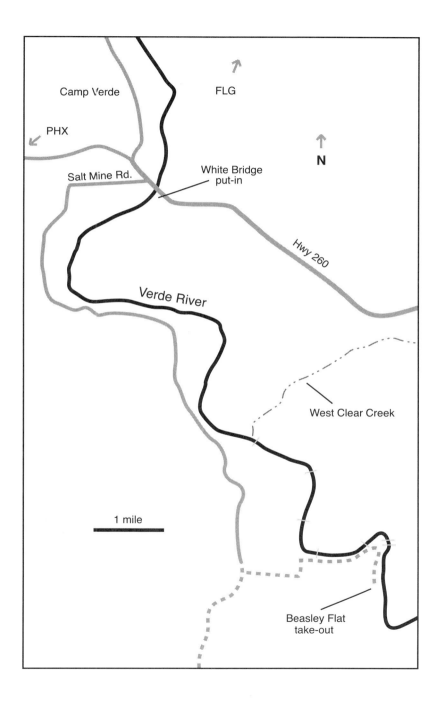

Woods Canyon

This is a fantastic two-day class V creek in a dramatic canyon. The only thing preventing it from being a real Arizona classic is a mandatory low water paddle-out of the lower reaches.

The problem lies in the timing of the dynamic daily snowmelt cycle. A typical springtime flow regime for a Woods run is a daily 300 cfs to 700 cfs cycle on the Dry Beaver Creek gage. The highest water of this 24-hour melt/freeze period usually reaches the lower part of this run at night. During daylight hours, the rocky wide riverbed of lower Woods is often a paltry 300 cfs or less. I wouldn't launch during warm winter storms. Woods can run at up to several thousand cfs at the put-in, and the record at the take-out is over 25,000 cfs. Better to run Woods on snowmelt during sunny spring weather. If you are willing to suffer through the rock bashing of the lower end, an awesome class V trip awaits.

The put-in is located where I-17 goes over the creek about 23 miles south of Flagstaff. The first two miles below here contain a couple of sieves, but it is mostly small boulders and grass hummocks creating class III-IV whitewater. The gradient quickly ramps up as basaltic waterfalls flow into teacup pools. A major side canyon enters from the south about 2.7 miles below the put-in. There are a few class IV-V rapids immediately below this side creek, then the canyon narrows and you'll arrive at a large falls coined Adrenaline Hangover.

Harlan Taney and Roy Lippman were the first to run this 70-foot sliding falls. Then both paddlers proceeded to pin within the next half mile, obviously succumbing to adrenaline hangovers following the falls. On the first descent of Woods, Eric Brown and I made a nerve-wracking portage around the falls across the snow slope on the left.

Below the falls, the riverbed is steep and somewhat sievey for the next quarter mile. Most of it is runnable, but portaging the entire section is often faster than scouting and paddling. This section completes the steepest mile of the run, coming in at 400 fpm. Even though the steepest stuff is behind you, the crux is still ahead.

The Coconino Sandstone periodically walls in the creek for much of the next 2.5 miles, making things rather committing. There is only one spot, however, where no portage route exists at normal levels. We call this rapid Mandatory Penalty, as it is difficult to run without at least grazing the right wall. Just below here, a creek comes shooting out of a narrows on the right, and things mellow briefly before several more drops lead down to the red Supai formation.

Not long after seeing the red rocks at river level, you'll arrive at a spectacular Supai gorge with a couple dicey rapids and one great drop that will likely push you into the right wall before you back-ender out the bottom. There is more pool-drop action below here, including Slide Rock On Steroids— a five-tiered flume of rippin' whitewater encased in a red rock narrows.

The last of the Supai rapids are just below, and the whitewater gradually starts to relent over the next couple of miles. There is one nasty undercut basalt rapid to watch out for here. The only other especially funky spot is an undercut sandstone ledge on river left. This is located somewhere on the paddle-out, when you'll be cruising.

The total run is about 18 miles. The gradient for the first 8 miles, which is the meat of the run, reads like this: 120, 160, 240, 300, 220, 240, 200, 160. Enjoy!!

Rattlesnake Canyon

Rattlesnake Canyon goes under Interstate 17 near the Stoneman Lake interchange about 30 miles south of Flagstaff. It is hardly even a recognizable watercourse here as most of us zoom past at 80 mph. However, Rattlesnake forms a deep canyon just downstream from the freeway before emptying into Woods Canyon.

The first descent of Rattlesnake occurred in the winter of 1995 when Dugald Bremner and Allen Haden spearheaded a run. They arrived at the put-in to find a second posse of paddlers including BJ Boyle, Eric Brown, Bill Morse, and Mark Thatcher. The six of them launched together at the regrettably late hour of noon, having delayed somewhat intentionally to allow for the water to rise.

The first two miles of the canyon consists of a basalt-choked riverbed dropping 160 fpm and 180 fpm respectively. Steady progress was made until the pace slowed in mile three, where the gradient picks up to 300 fpm—the steepest of the run. Following a portage, Thatcher, a diabetic, noticed his blood sugar at an all-time low. He and Boyle prudently left the gorge via a trail that once serviced a now defunct gage. This escape route comes in just above a 30-foot waterfall, which was portaged on the left. (It has since been run.)

Following the lengthy portage, everyone suddenly realized that their short winter day was rapidly coming to an end. Three miles of steep creek (240 fpm, 240 fpm, 180 fpm) remained, followed by a three mile "paddle out" on flooding Woods Canyon. The boys must've put their bombing shoes on, because they made the confluence of Woods by dark. Bremner took the lead by Braille at that point, and the foursome somehow made the take-out without any disasters.

Rattlesnake is tough to catch, even by Arizona standards. I have only been there at an optimal level once, and we didn't have the attitude for it that day. I painted a gage at the downstream end of the tunnel beneath the freeway, but it is pretty worthless. Your best bet is to go right after a big flood, and eyeball it at the put-in at I-17. Take out on Route 179 where the highway crosses Dry Beaver Creek.

Verde River
(Beasley to Gap Creek or Childs)

General Description: The standard whitewater run of northern Arizona
Difficulty: III (IV)
Gradient: 20 fpm
Length: 8 miles to Gap Creek, 16 miles to Childs
Flow: minimum: 300 cfs (150 cfs for low-water boating)
    ideal: 800 — 2,000 cfs
Gage: Verde River near Camp Verde.
Shuttle: 11.5 miles from Beasley to Gap, rough dirt road, marginally bikeable / It's about 38 miles from Beasley to Childs, dirt road
Elevation: 2,950'—2,610'
Likely Season: February, March, April, occasional spikes during monsoon season from July to mid-September
Peak Flow: Camp Verde gage—119,000 cfs February 20, 1993.

This stretch of the Verde, along with the upper Salt, are the two most commonly run whitewater rivers in Arizona (excluding Grand Canyon of course). There are two take-outs for this section of the Verde, one at Gap Creek eight miles down, and another at Childs sixteen miles down.

If you are looking for the most whitewater with the least shuttle, the Gap Creek take-out is for you, but there is a catch. You'll have to carry your boat a half-mile uphill along a narrow trail before reaching your shuttle rig and any hope of cold beer. So, for rafts, canoes, and any boats that are not easily carried, the Childs take-out farther downstream is the best choice.

A Childs take-out allows riverside parking. There is also a nice hot spring about a mile upstream, across the river from the parking area. Paddling all the way to Childs offers several class II and III rapids, and a remote river corridor suitable for camping. Given the long shuttle, a two-day trip is not a bad idea here.

Most of the memorable whitewater on the Verde, however, is located in the first few miles below Beasley Flat. The first big sweeping right turn signals the first significant rapid—Off the Wall. This is a fast sluice against ledges with some powerful reactionary waves. More class II and III leads to a gentle left bend where basalt flows span the riverbed, creating Verde Falls.

This is the biggest rapid on the Verde, a class IV with a pre-falls and a fast cliffed-in run-out below the drop. At high water (over 2,000 cfs) the falls are a big juicy flush. At low levels (below 500 cfs), the only line is a bony double drop on the right. During moderate flows, there is usually a clean boof line over the ledge on the left.

Below the falls the water is swift for the next half mile or so with a couple distinct drops and good surf spots. Then the river mellows into long pools separated by occasional class II and III gravel bars. Palisades and Bull

Whitewater Rivers 165

A Prescott College group charges Verde Falls at high water

Run are the standout rapids, the latter containing a surf hole at the bottom.

The last big rapid before Gap Creek is Punk Rock. Plenty of paddlers have forcefully been taught the meaning of "ferry angle" at this rapid, and unwillingly slam danced with the large boulder that gives the rapid its name.

Gap Creek is only about a mile farther. This take-out can be identified by a grove of cottonwood and sycamore trees high on the right hillside. The actual take-out beach is located upstream from this grove, just above where Gap Creek hits the river. If you run Bushmans, a rapid with a great surf wave over 1,500 cfs, you've gone too far.

Once below Gap Creek, the hardest rapids of the run are behind you, but there are still several boulder-strewn class II and III drops. The ever-present tree obstructions of the Verde remain a factor as well. The scenery and camping are good. Look for a concrete structure on river right just above the Childs power plant. This is Verde Hot Springs, and during times of high water paddlers are likely to have it to themselves.

There is a detailed river guide for this section of the Verde available from the Tonto National Forest. Check out their website at www.fs.fed.us/r3/tonto/home.shtml and look for the Verde River Guide link.

Logistics: To reach the Beasley Flat put-in, take Salt Mine Road off Highway 260 in Camp Verde. This is located on river right near the white bridge south of downtown. Follow Salt Mine Road 8.8 miles (it turns to dirt here) and turn left. Staying on the main road, it is 2.4 miles farther to Beasley Flat.

To get to the Gap Creek take-out, return to Salt Mine Road at the Beasley Flat turn, and continue south. It is several long, bumpy, and sometimes impassably muddy miles down road #574 to the small shaded parking area on Gap Creek.

For the Childs take-out, return to Highway 260, and follow it east about 7 miles to road #708. Follow the signs to Childs from here. It is about 15 miles to the intersection of road #502 where you'll turn right, then several more miles to Childs. The road is narrow and winding as it switchbacks into the river canyon above Childs. Like the Gap Creek road, it can be a mess when wet.

Whitewater Rivers 167

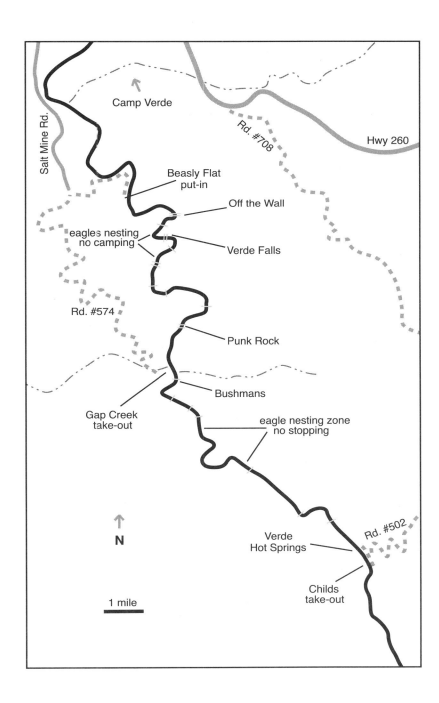

Upper Verde
(Perkinsville - TAPCO)

The Verde below Perkinsville runs through a scenic canyon in an obscure and little-visited part of the Verde watershed. Here the river cuts through Redwall Limestone, and at times it seems as if you are paddling through a side arm of Grand Canyon.

I counted five class III rapids on the run, plus one sieve that is a sharp but runnable class IV with enough water, and a portage at low water. This crux rapid comes adjacent to a railroad tunnel about halfway through the run. The biggest hazards on this section aren't the rapids, however, but the many trees that encroach on the small river in the first few miles below Perkinsville. At high water, it could get scary.

An ideal level for advanced paddlers is 300 to 400 cfs, although most descents have occurred with much less water. With flows less than 300 cfs, the 20 miles can create a very long day. The semi-long shuttle doesn't help matters, although driving along the north side of Mingus Mtn. with views of red rocks and the San Francisco Peaks makes for possibly the most spectacular shuttle drive in the state.

For more information, consult Jim Singluff's Verde Recreation Guide, if you can find a copy. He has a detailed description of this beautiful and off-the-beaten-path run.

Wet Beaver Creek

Wet Beaver Creek is one of the principal streams draining the western Mogollon Rim. The drainages to the north and south of Wet Beaver (Woods and West Clear) are both excellent multi-day whitewater adventures. Wet Beaver, too, seems likely to be a great run. But it is not to be.

Wet Beaver is full of trees. A perennial flow of about 8 cfs keeps this creek's riparian vegetation quite healthy, and the drainage isn't big enough to ream out the river channel with sizeable floods. The result is a creekbed thick with vegetation. Lower Wet Beaver, however, does have a run that is suitable for class III paddlers who are looking for something new.

I once put-in at the golf course in Rimrock, and paddled down to the confluence with Dry Beaver Creek. I was a beginning paddler at the time, launching solo, so I was pretty pumped-up. I didn't own a paddling jacket, and it was a chilly gray day, so I was bundled in fleece and wool with a ski jacket duct-taped at the wrists to serve as my "waterproof" layer. Between my bulky wardrobe and my excitement for the run, I launched without thinking to put on my lifejacket. It was only after I paddled the run, hitchhiked the shuttle, and returned to my truck that I saw my new pfd, to my surprise, sitting proudly on the front seat.

I recall a few class II rapids and a handful of strainers to keep you on your toes. It is not stunning scenery or wilderness, but it is a nice riverine environment away from the road.

Hell Canyon
(Little Hell Canyon bridge – Hell Canyon bridge)

When the upper Verde watershed is really cranking, this creekbed draining the south side of Bill Williams Mountain sometimes gets enough flow to paddle.

We put in at Little Hell Canyon Lake. Immediately after floating through the tunnel under the highway, there are two class IV-V basalt drops. This is the biggest whitewater on the run, and it is easy to put in below both rapids. The next quarter mile is a brush-fest, and you might be wondering about the feasibility of paddling this cow ditch, but then things open up and a nice class III creek presents itself. About three miles down, Meath Wash comes in on the right, often doubling the flow (boosting it to 500 cfs on our run).

The scenery consists of low basalt cliffs, and a thick pygmy forest of juniper and scrub oak. Redwall Limestone emerges about halfway through the run, and it is this Redwall canyon that you will climb out of at the takeout. The last rapid visible from the highway bridge is one of the most treefilled on the entire run, so don't get discouraged based on this view.

One could continue below the highway and on to the Verde for a takeout at Perkinsville, but the roads on this shuttle would likely be quite muddy if Hell Canyon is running. Brad Dimock and Wayne Van Voorhies ran this lower stretch down to the Verde in the early '80s. Dimock reports the character to be similar to the upper run.

Verde River
wilderness run
(Childs – Horseshoe Reservoir)

General Description: A small wilderness desert river
Difficulty: II (III)
Gradient: 18 fpm
Length: 30 miles
Flow: minimum: 150 cfs at Camp Verde gage
ideal: 400 — 1,000 cfs
Gage: Verde River near Camp Verde / Verde River below Tangle Creek
Shuttle: Sheep Bridge take-out: 93 miles, pavement and 30+ miles of rough dirt / Horseshoe take-out: 124 miles, pavement and 9 miles of graded dirt
Elevation: 2,600' — 2,000'
Likely Season: February — April
Peak Flow: Camp Verde gage—119,000 cfs February 19, 1993. Tangle Creek gage—150,000 cfs February 24, 1891.

Below the lonely outpost of Childs, the Verde runs through the heart of central Arizona wilderness. This is a land of rugged canyons, saguaro cactus, floodplains of mesquite, and hidden mountain springs. Black bears and mountain lions roam the area, and river otters swim beneath the ripples of the river. A Verde wilderness float is a classic Southwestern trip.

A couple miles below Childs, the first significant tributary—Fossil Creek—enters on the left. The Verde continues to grow as it enters the most northeasterly extension of the great Sonoran Desert. A few bends below Fossil, the East Verde River comes in, followed by Houston Creek on the right.

The biggest hazards on the water are tree-lined channels of swift water. Sometimes a random log falls into the current, creating a potentially dangerous strainer. The Verde is littered with twisted remnants of pinned canoes. Keep it straight and watch out for those trees!

The camping is adequate to good throughout the river corridor. Sand and gravel beaches provide water's edge accommodations, while rich green mesquite flats offer shade and high water sleeping spots.

In case of emergency, a trail follows river left for much of the run. In some places it is quite a distance from the river, but once found, it leads to Sheep Bridge where a crossing to river right can be made. There are numerous other hiking options from the Verde as well, with routes leading into the wild and rocky Mazatzal Mountains.

At high water, the distance from Childs to Horseshoe Reservoir can be covered in a long day. This is rarely done, however, and making a speed run down the Verde is missing the point. Most groups take three or four days, allowing for some relaxation time in camp, or even a side hike. At

Whitewater Rivers 171

A common Verde ornament

low water levels, a five day trip or more is not unreasonable.

Before setting out, check out the Tonto National Forest Verde River Guide. This offers more details than are listed here, and indicates which areas are closed for eagle protection.

Logistics: There are two take-out options for a Verde wilderness trip: Sheep Bridge and Horseshoe Reservoir. Sheep Bridge is the first road access along the river, and makes for the shortest shuttle. There are a couple drawbacks, however. When the Agua Fria River is running high (this is rare), the Bloody Basin Road crossing leading to Sheep Bridge is treacherous or impossible. If you make it across the Agua Fria, it is about 30 miles of rocky, slow dirt road to the river. For the Sheep Bridge take-out, exit I-17 at Bloody Basin Road, exit #259, then follow road #269, following the signs to Sheep Bridge and the Verde River.

The Horseshoe Reservoir take-out is reached via relatively tame roads, but it is a longer drive, and requires an extra 5 miles of paddling across the reservoir if it is full. To reach the take-out at Horseshoe, exit I-17 at Carefree Highway, exit #223. Head east for several miles to the town of Cave Creek, and follow Cave Creek Road northeast out of town to Bartlett Dam Road. Follow Bartlett Dam Road for 6.3 miles, and turn north onto Horseshoe Dam Road (road #225). It is 11 miles from here to the launch ramp / take-out at Horseshoe Reservoir. The first 2 miles of Horseshoe Dam Road are paved, then it is graded dirt.

Whitewater Rivers 173

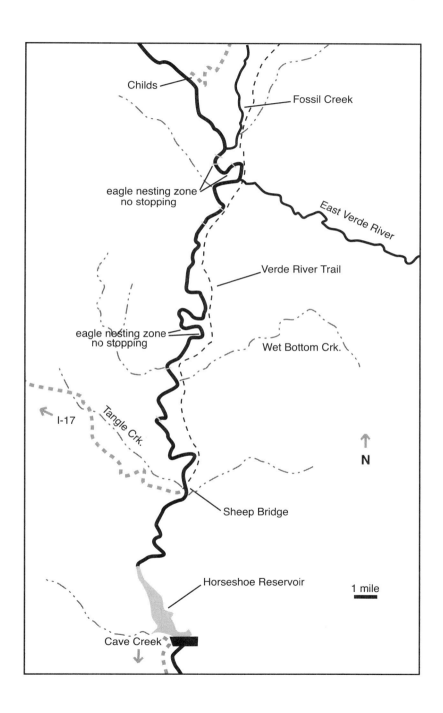

West Clear Creek
(wilderness run)

West Clear Creek is an awesome class V wilderness run. As of this writing, there has been only one full descent of this Arizona gem, and for that reason it is not listed as a featured run in this book. It is, however, a Southwestern classic that should be on every expedition boater's to-do list.

The first few miles are a meandering mountain creek in the forest with small tributaries slowly notching up the flow. Several miles into the run, the whitewater picks up dramatically with a steep IV+ rapid as the creek cuts through Kaibab Limestone. Shortly thereafter, the Coconino Sandstone arrives. This rock layer, the most daunting formation to kayaking throughout the Mogollon Rim region, dominates West Clear Creek for the next 15 miles.

The first gorge cutting through the Coconino is also the steepest at 250 fpm. This Willow Valley Gorge (so named because the stream is called Willow Valley Creek at this point) contains several committing class V rapids, and one 30-foot sliding falls that has yet to be run. Rock climbing is needed to scout some of the rapids, and portaging would be slow and difficult. As the Willow Valley Gorge relents, a 100 fpm section of class IV eases into a couple miles of class II leading to the confluence of Clover Creek.

A few more miles of flatwater gives you some time to relax and marvel at the soaring sandstone cliffs and majestic fir trees that define the canyon. But the respite doesn't last long.

Class III and IV pool-drop with the occasional log portage characterizes the next few miles. The gradient steepens as basalt boulder gardens invade the riverbed, bringing about a mile of fantastic class IV — IV+ rapids.

This fun read-and-run section comes to a screeching halt with the arrival of Commitment Drop. Here the Coconino Sandstone returns, pinching the creek between vertical walls, with a waterfall serving as entrance to the box canyon. A lengthy scout involving some climbing commences here, one of several rock climbing scouts required on the run. Assuming the gorge appears clean, Commitment Drop will lead to a mile of narrow canyon scenery and moderate whitewater as the creek bends south. When the creek turns west again, get out your scouting shoes, because The Gauntlet is next.

This long rapid trapped between vertical cliff walls is probably the most dramatic whitewater scene I have ever paddled. At the bottom, it dumps you out into a rock enclosed pool known among canyoneering enthusiasts as The White Box. You can breathe a small sigh of relief at this point, because the most committing Coconino narrows are behind you, but the red Supai formation has plenty in store.

The next six miles are a series of spectacularly playful class V Supai mini-gorges interspersed with less playful slot canyons and a few mellow boulder rapids. Curtain Falls—a 15-footer of nuthin' but love is one of the last drops before the creek starts to mellow into the 5 mile paddle out.

Lisa Gelczis, Josh Lowry, and I ran West Clear in April of 1998. We took three days, which seemed just perfect. Jon Hirsch hiked into the middle section with a young and ambitious female partner named Morning Glory a couple weeks after our descent. Hirsch and Morning Glory had lower water and used inflatable kayaks. They ran the crux Gauntlet section, then hiked out with their boats!

Total distance is about 35 miles. The put-in is the bridge over Willow Valley Creek on FH3 (Lake Mary Road) between Happy Jack and Clints Well. Take-out is Bull Pen Ranch Campground near Camp Verde.

A perfect water level seems to be around 500 cfs. We launched on about 250 cfs when the gage at the lower end was coming off a spike of 2,000 cfs. At the take-out, the gage was reading 500 cfs, which is the flow we had for most of the run. The best time to catch West Clear is in the spring when there is copious snowmelt. Unfortunately, the drainage often floods away with rain on snow in February and March during wet winters. The canyon is way too narrow and cold to run in winter, with probable ice. Mid-March during warm sunny weather is the earliest I would go. April is best.

Lower West Clear Creek

West Clear Creek below Bull Pen Campground is a class III run for class IV boaters. There are plenty of trees encroaching on the riverbed that could present real problems at high water. We ran it at 500 cfs, and this seemed like a good level.

The creek flows through a basalt canyon with nice class II and III rapids. On our trip, we saw several black tailed hawks. The take-out is at the Highway 260 bridge unless you decide to continue down to the Verde.

Fossil Creek

General Description: A travertine riverbed with a year-round boatable flow
Difficulty: III—IV
Gradient: 140 fpm
Length: 2 to 6 miles
Flow: minimum: 46 cfs
      ideal: 300 — 500 cfs
Gage: No gage as of 2007. The base flow is stable. To estimate Fossil's flow during runoff events, figure 30%—40% of West Clear Creek's flow.
Shuttle: Middle Falls to Powerhouse Falls: 1.5 miles, hiking / Fossil Springs to #708 bridge: 9 miles, 6 driving on dirt, then 3 hiking downhill
Elevation: 4,300'—3,700'
Likely Season: Anytime for base flow runs. February or March for higher water
Peak Flow: 10,000 cfs (estimated)

Travertine rivers are some of the most spectacular whitewater playgrounds in the world. Mexico's Jatate', Agua Azul, and Santa Maria are classics, and Grand Canyon's Little Colorado River and Havasu Creek are highlights for hiking and swimming. Warm water, picturesque falls, and deep marine pools make these rivers famous. Fossil Creek is another splendid travertine river, an Arizona treasure.

Fossil Creek emanates from Fossil Springs, an idyllic oasis that produces about 40 cfs of warm clear water year-round. For much of the 20th century, this water was diverted into an aqueduct and sent downstream to the Irving and Childs power plants, effectively de-watering the creek. In 2005, however, the diversion was decommissioned, bringing life back to Fossil Creek.

I heard rumors of people boating on Fossil Creek shortly after the water was restored to the riverbed. Honestly, I had a hard time imagining that there was enough water to actually paddle here. "Forty cfs?" I thought, "my God these people are desperate!" Well, wasn't I in for a pleasant surprise.

Fossil Creek at base flow is a blast! Yes, it is very low water boating, you will get stuck often, and paddlers from more saturated regions will scratch their heads upon seeing the diminutive creek, but a run here at base flow is still totally worth it. The water is luxuriously warm and clear, the travertine falls offer beautiful scenery, and the whitewater is surprisingly good.

The entire creek, from the springs to the Verde, has been run at base flow. The section from the springs to Middle Falls is full of strainers. Below Powerhouse Falls, shallow travertine dams dominate the creek until the road #708 bridge. Below the road #708 bridge there is one good set of rapids called The Ghetto, then it's predominantly brushy and bony to the Verde.

The heart of the run is from Middle Falls to Powerhouse Falls. This is the section I recommend at base flow. Middle Falls is a 20-footer into a big blue pool. You can climb above the drop and start your run with a bang, or put-in at the pool below.

The next mile is a series of travertine slides, chutes, and ledges which get progressively cleaner as you travel downstream. With only about 50 cfs, the pin potential isn't huge, nor are the holes very intimidating. Still, there is enough gradient in many of the drops that you could get mangled if you are in the wrong place, and precise moves are sometimes necessary. Standout rapids include Slot Machine (don't get sucked left into the overhanging wall of travertine), and Paralyzer, where it looks like you'll piton

Running travertine ledges on Fossil Creek

the rock, but a kind pillow bounces you around.

The grand finale to the run comes at Powerhouse Falls. These falls are split by an island, and both sides have been run. The right is easier, featuring a curving slide. The left is a steep double drop ending with a 5-foot boof. Stay clear of private living quarters and work areas at the power plant when taking out below Powerhouse.

Now some more notes...Fossil at base flow is only feasible with small boats. For kayaks, something less than 7 feet long is best. It is just too tiny of a creek for anything much larger. Small open boats might work well here also, as they draw very little water. Inflatable kayaks might work too, the narrower the better. Whatever the boat, buoyancy is key. The travertine is always growing, floods will periodically alter this dynamic river channel, and the rapids will always be changing.

The first time I ran Fossil, it was in winter following a big flood. We hiked down the Fossil Springs Trail and launched above the springs on about 400 cfs. We portaged the dam located below the springs, and continued all the way to the road #708 bridge for about a 7-mile run. In the first few miles near the springs, there are some class IV rapids (one IV+) and some log hazards, along with lots of class III boulder rapids. I recommend this entire section if you have the water.

One more thing...Remember to pack a garbage bag when you visit Fossil. Disrespectful masses tend to flock here during weekends, leaving a trail of pollution in wheir wake. Help maintain the integrity of the creek by cleaning up what you can.

Logistics: There is trailhead parking for Fossil Creek on the north side of road #708. This is a mile east of the road #708 bridge, a few hundred yards upstream from Powerhouse Falls and the power plant, and about 11 miles west and 2,000 feet below Strawberry, Arizona.

To reach Middle Falls from the trailhead, hike up road #708 a couple hundred yards to a blockaded old spur road heading left near a spring. This old road will soon narrow into a trail that leads to Middle Falls. The route splits a few times, but most spurs re-connect before long. The last section before reaching the falls leads through a creek-side riparian forest. Another route to Middle Falls crosses the creek at the parking area and leads upstream on river right.

For launching at Fossil Springs, hike downhill on the Fossil Springs Trail for 3 miles. The trailhead is at the top of the canyon, 6 miles from the road #708 bridge over Fossil Creek.

Whitewater Rivers 179

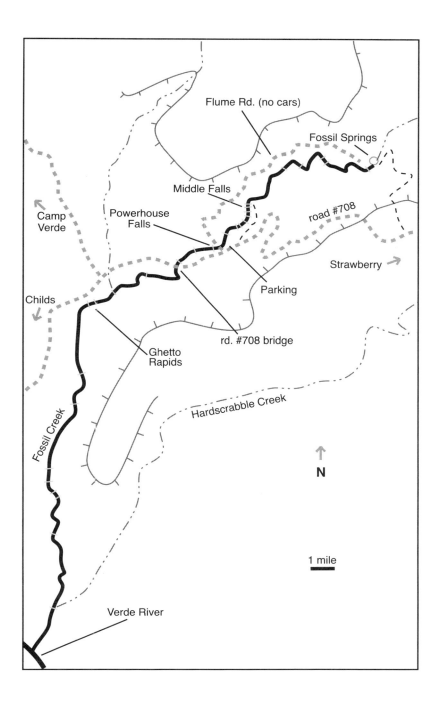

Lower Verde
(Horseshoe – Salt River)

The lower Verde should be a standard Arizona run. It is near the Valley of the Sun, it has regular boatable flows, and it is a rich riparian corridor in the desert. However, access to the lower Verde is problematic. There are sensitive eagle nesting sites adjacent to the river, and every logical run is hampered by long shuttles or property restrictions. Because of these issues, the lower Verde is not a featured river in this book. Still, there are a couple sections of the lower Verde that I feel compelled to mention here.

The most logical run on the lower Verde is between Horseshoe and Bartlett Reservoirs. One could put in below Horseshoe Dam (refer to the Horseshoe Reservoir description for directions, and launch at the campground below the spillway overlook), and continue to Bartlett Lake. There is one nasty corner rapid that collects strainers where the river curves beneath the road about a mile below the dam. Other than that, this section is typical Verde: grassy banks, class I and II cobble bar rapids, big flat pools, and overhanging cottonwoods.

About 2.5 miles below Horseshoe, there is an eagle nesting closure area on both sides of the river. Stay on the water to observe these great birds, and make sure to not disturb them. The closed area ends at Devils Hole where an old 4WD road comes in on the right. Below here the river bends east, and depending on water level, enters Bartlett Reservoir.

The last 6 miles (about half the total distance of the run) of the Horseshoe to Bartlett section is on Bartlett Lake, so allow ample time to paddle the flatwater at the end of the day. The take-out is at Bartlett Flat, located about 4 miles up-lake from Bartlett Dam Road. Total shuttle distance from Horseshoe to Bartlett Flat is about 21 miles. There is a $6 fee per day to park at Bartlett Flat.

There is no gage for the Horseshoe to Bartlett stretch of the Verde, but if Horseshoe Reservoir is near full, chances are that the river will be running. Good levels are 200 to 500 cfs.

Below Bartlett Reservoir, the Verde enters a scenic and roadless corridor for a few miles before emerging near Needle Rock Recreation Area. This Bartlett to Needle Rock run could be a nice float, but the shuttle is a ridiculous 50 miles, and the entire section lies within an eagle closure, so there is no stopping once you launch.

Below the Needle Rock area, the eagle closure remains on river left, but there are some access points on river right. From Camp Creek Wash to Box Bar Ford, the river contains several class I gravel bars. This is a nice desert river with profligate herons and kingfishers. There is a gage for this part of the river too, titled Verde River below Bartlett on the USGS streamflow page. One can launch at Camp Creek Wash, located 0.7 miles north of Needle Rock Recreation Area on forest road #20. To reach the take-out at Box Bar Ford, start on road #20 at the north end of the Rio Verde development, then take road #2150 east for 0.4 miles to road #160. Turn left toward the river, and Box Bar Ford is 0.4 miles farther.

Below this point, the Verde enters the Fort McDowell Indian Reservation, and access is restricted. The Verde rolls along for about 15 more miles before joining the Salt River just a couple miles above Granite Reef Dam.

The lower Verde runs through rugged desert near Phoenix

Agua Fria River
(the gorge)

General Description: A long class V day run with a granite riverbed.
Difficulty: IV+ — V
Gradient: 66 fpm/gorge gradient...70,100,160,120,120,90...
Length: 17 miles
Flow: minimum: 100 cfs
ideal: 300 — 500 cfs
*These flows correlate with the Mayer gage. Actual flows are often a little higher.
Gage: Agua Fria River near Mayer. There is also a gage near Rock Springs, but this gage is not very helpful since it is below the take-out, and below the confluence of a tributary almost equal in size to the Agua Fria. During periods of vast fluctuation, the Mayer gage seems to not reflect the actual flow in the canyon. I once ran the river when this gage was indicating 81 cfs, but the actual flow seemed like 200 cfs.
Shuttle: 23 miles, mostly hitchable
Elevation: 3,300'—2,200'
Likely Season: Following heavy rain. This usually occurs in winter, but can also happen in summer. Runs have been made in January, February, March, and September.
Peak Flow: Mayer gage—33,100 cfs February 19, 1980. Rock Springs gage—85,000 cfs November 27, 1919.

I consider the Agua Fria to be the best one-day run in Arizona. The river snakes through a beautiful desert canyon covered in Saguaro cactus. The shuttle is easy. Trees and strainers, although present, are less of a hazard than on most Arizona rivers. On top of all this, the Agua Fria has a California-esque riverbed of polished granite that forms complex and fun whitewater.

Not that you'll be seeing any of this whitewater for the first couple miles of the run. Things start out flat and shallow—your warm-up strokes will be made avoiding gravel bars and the occasional nest of willow trees. The action starts about three miles below the put-in with some class III boulder gardens. At four miles, the first saguaro cactus appears, along with class IV rapids.

There are two significant drops here that are a good sampling of what is to come. The first is a short double drop with a launchpad in the left channel. The other is a broad ledge usually run down the chutes on the right.

Four and a half miles in, Badger Spring Wash enters on the right. Look for this trickling side creek at a pool just before the river turns left. This is a good place to regroup and assess things, because it is your last easy option for hiking out. It is a simple 0.5 mile walk up the sandy (beware of quicksand and mud) wash to a parking area, and another mile from here to the freeway. When short on time, one can also put in here.

Whitewater Rivers 183

Running the falls on the Agua Fria

Below Badger Spring Wash, the Agua Fria begins its turbulent boulder-choked journey off Black Mesa to the desert floor. Most of the rapids are class IV and IV+, but several class V's seem to be perfectly placed to keep you on your toes. A class V boater will have a great time on this run. An adventurous class IV boater will be gripped.

The first rapid of note below Badger Spring Wash is Maelstrom, where a steep glassy tongue leads into an agitated mess of converging currents. Dugald's Mystery Ledge is the next biggie. On my first run in 1993, BJ Boyle and I watched in amazement as Dugald Bremner disapeared in a hole here for a full second before surfacing and paddling out. This rapid takes higher flows to become runnable. It is usually the one mandatory portage on the run. A mile farther is Rail Slide—a complex class V that sometimes sends paddlers sliding down a fin of granite against the right wall. Just after the canyon makes a 90 degree right turn at Perry Tank Creek, you'll arrive at a 20-foot waterfall with a boulder sitting just beyond the backwash at its base.

Less than a half mile below the falls is Double Boof—you'll know when you're there. I always breathe a little easier once past Double Boof, even though three miles of chutes, slides, slots and rocks remain. The more memorable drops are Poop Chute (where a river right channel barely wider than a kayak avoids the hole of the main stream), and Idiot Proof Boof, featuring a perfect diving board launchpad. When you sense things starting to mellow, brace yourself for a final flurry of action. The big rapid down here is Low Blood Sugar, named after an ill-advised attempt to finish the canyon without a lunch break. Run correctly, it requires some rock dancing at the top before zooming around a blind corner to the left of a giant boulder.

Below Low Blood Sugar, things soon drop off to class III and then you are officially on the paddle out. Wake up calls come in the form of rollicking class III rapids (and one class IV) but these only occasionally punctuate the drudgery of the long flat pools. Paddling through the broad lower canyon in the golden afternoon light, you'll be glad you got an early start. A 9:00 a.m. launch is appropriate for this run. A noon put-in on the Agua Fria is likely to get you be-nighted.

If you are behind schedule, there are some options. Rather than facing an I-17 hitchhike in the dark, we once took out at the side canyon leading to the Sunset Point rest area. There is a trail here, but it is a tough and muddy 3 miles to the freeway.

Logistics: The take-out for the Agua Fria is in Black Canyon City. You can take out where the main road in town crosses the river, or upstream at a vacant industrial area. To get here, take exit #244 off I-17 at Black Canyon City and head southeast from the freeway for 0.8 miles, then go left on Coldwater Canyon Road. Make your way upstream and you'll arrive at the take-out 1.8 miles from the Coldwater Canyon turn.

For the put-in, return to I-17 and head up the hill to Bloody Basin Road—exit #259. Take Bloody Basin Road 5.3 miles to the Agua Fria.

Whitewater Rivers 185

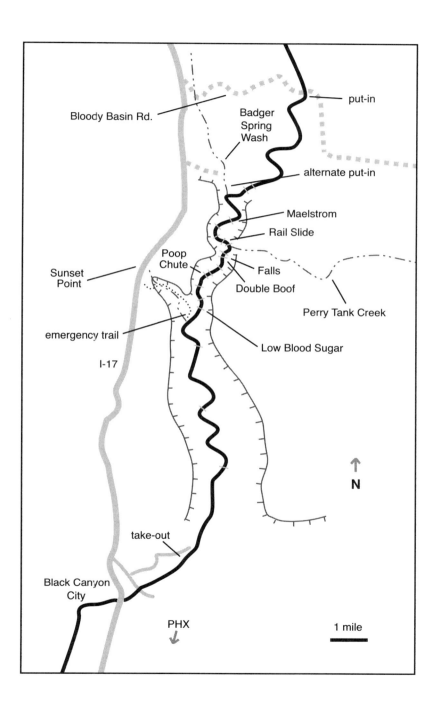

Black Canyon
(Cleator to Bumble Bee)

In the winter of 2005, Gilbert paddler Aaron Riding led the initial charge on this nice class III creek in the desert. The first couple of miles are swift class II in a narrow channel. With higher flows (over 2,000 cfs at Rock Springs), the small creek jumps up a full grade in difficulty, and this first section turns into a fast class III romp where a swim could easily get out of hand. The rapids get more defined as gray igneous rock pinches down on the creek. The highlight in this first section is a man made rock dam that forms a 4-foot vertical ledge.

Just less than halfway through the run, Poland Creek comes in on the right, normally doubling the flow. The riverbed broadens somewhat, and boulder gardens become the most common rapid type. There are a few standout play features, and many more waves that are worth a quick ride. A few mines sit on the banks, but the undisturbed Sonoran Desert is the main scenic feature of this lovely desert creek. There is another 10-mile section downstream of Bumble Bee Creek that is reportedly similar, but with slightly less gradient.

To reach the take-out, take the Bumble Bee exit off I-17, and follow the road north toward Bumble Bee. In about 2 miles, the road turns to dirt. In another 3 miles, turn left onto a secondary dirt road heading toward the creek. This turn is before the main road crosses Bumble Bee Creek. It is about 0.3 rough miles down to Black Canyon Creek from the main road. For the put-in, continue north on the main road for 8.3 miles to the bridge over the creek near Cleator.

Poland Creek

Poland Creek is a major tributary of Black Canyon, cutting an impressive, steep granite canyon out of the Bradshaw Mountains. Jim McComb and posse first paddled a class III-IV section on lower Poland, accessing via a 4WD road on creek left. I had hiked much of the upper creek, and considered it too small and steep for kayaking. Enter Cody Howard.

Following some pre-dawn starts that revealed a trickle of water and the occasional dead cow in the creek, Cody and gang finally caught the creek with water in the winter of 2008, and discovered a top-notch class V run.

Despite an early start, the group was forced to bivouac in the canyon (excessive scouting and filming were the reported culprits), most of them without sleeping bags. Nontheless, in the morning they pushed onward, ran many big drops, and reached the take-out. For some quality footage of haggard paddlers following a be-nighting, check out Cody's film: *The Risen Sun*. There is great Poland Creek whitewater action in the movie too.

Your best bet for a gage is to simply be there early in the morning when everything in the area is running, and have a look. Binoculars might help. The put-in is a 1,000-foot vertical hike down trail #225, located at a turnout near milepost #25 a few miles east of Crown King. The take-out is at the end of the only road leading south from Cleator, located just west of the Cleator Bar. Fork right when in doubt. The run is about 5 miles long, with an average gradient around 300 fpm.

Turkey Creek

This is the main upper arm of Black Canyon. Pat Phillips, West Howland, and I ran it in 2008 following an epic 4WD shuttle that finally ended at Bear Creek, a tributary. We launched here, and paddled a couple miles on 75 cfs (not too bad) to Turkey Creek, which looked brushy and small above here anyway. Downstream, we found several miles of nice class III and IV (one V?) in a wild desert canyon—a stellar run. We had roughly 400 cfs by the take-out, which seemed perfect. The run is about 8 miles long, with gradients around 150 fpm. The take-out is just north of Cleator.

Sycamore Creek
(Butterfly Canyon)

Sycamore Creek runs through a beautiful canyon adjacent to the Beeline Highway (hwy 87) between Scottsdale and Payson. The 7-mile run contains several high quality granite rapids, but also plenty of brush and some portages around sievey drops.

Pat Phillips and Eric Seifer did the first half of the run in 1993 before being shut down by a narrowing gorge and darkness. In 1998, Rob Rieterman's group shelved their Sycamore plans when they learned of a boy scout who had recently drowned in the creek. In 2005, Matt Fahey and I launched at the Sunflower bridge only to come across a pickup truck in the creek that contained two dead bodies. After alerting the sherrif, we finished two-thirds of the run before I pinned, swam, lost my paddle, and hiked out.

Finally, in February 2008 Pat Phillips and I made the first full descent, launching at 10 am, and taking out at dusk. We made 12 portages, a few of which were to save time. We were quite pleased with ourselves at having completed the run until Cody Howard and Mike Fisher ran it the next week with just 2 portages! I can't guess which two those were, because at least four drops in the canyon look equally bad to me.

It is only 7 miles from Sunflower to the Highway 87 take-out, but plan on a full day to cover this distance. The meat of the run is a 3-mile section with a gradient of 240 fpm. There are some fantastic clean sluices in polished granite, but many other drops are cluttered with trees.

A good level is approximately 300 cfs. The gage (Sycamore Creek near Ft. McDowell) is several miles below the run, so your best bet is to go to the take-out and have a look. If it looks bony here, it's good in the canyon.

East Verde
(Day stretch)

General Description: A varied and long wilderness day run in central Arizona
Difficulty: IV (V)
Gradient: 61 fpm. Both gorges are 120 fpm.
Length: 18 miles. This is normally done in one long day, but a two-day trip could be a nice option if flows are sustained.
Flow: minimum: 200 cfs—visual
 ideal: 300 — 600 cfs—visual
Gage: East Verde River near Childs. This gage is 35 miles downstream from the put-in, so its usefulness is limited. A visual estimate at the put-in is the best boater's gage here.
Shuttle: 20 miles, pavement and muddy dirt road
Elevation: 4,500'—3,400'
Likely Season: February, March
Peak Flow: Childs gage—23,500 cfs September 5, 1970

The East Verde drains the southern slope of the Mogollon Rim near the town of Payson, Arizona. Here the Rim is at its most magnificent as it sharply divides the Colorado Plateau to the north from the central Arizona mountains to the south. The fingertips of this river system tap snowy draws of Douglas fir growing under the shade of the Rim. The river cuts through walls of granite, and placidly drifts past groves of sycamores before finally merging with the main Verde River in the Sonoran Desert.

The most commonly paddled segment lies upstream from Doll Baby Ranch. Don't miss the take-out at Doll Baby. The next road access is two long days downstream—at Horseshoe Reservoir on the Verde. The put-in is a tad less remote. The first mile of paddling will take you through a riverside subdivision.

Not long after leaving the summer homes behind, you'll arrive at a 5-foot ledge of pink granite. This one will get you loosened up in time for the crux of the run which is lurking just downstream. The first class V rapid is called Magical Mushroom Forest—so coined by a fellow called Jake the Snake who led the first raft descent of the East Verde, but that's another story. A maze of trees complicate the first half of the rapid, and a delicate move to the right of a pin-prone slot completes the run.

Immediately below here lies the pink gorge—a short but beautiful series of three big drops through bedrock. The first falls has a class IV lead-in to a large nasty-looking pourover. The lengthy but simple portage is on the right. Just below this is Chunchee Falls (don't pull a Chunchee), a juicy waterfall slide. The third rapid in the series is a heinous slot that is always portaged (left), although high water might open a line. A class IV rapid serves as the exit from the pink gorge.

The Pink Gorge of the East Verde

For the next few miles, the river tumbles along in a delightful series of class III and IV rapids. Eventually things smooth out and it behooves paddlers to assume a downriver pace or a dark take-out could be looming.

If your group is falling behind schedule, there is an oxbow portage on the lower end of the run that can save an hour or more. This portage comes a few bends after North Peak is visible downstream. Following a few good class IV drops in gray bedrock, the river makes a 180 degree right turn with prominent Tapeats Sandstone cliffs emerging on river left. Look for the trail on the left, just above a small rapid on the outside of the bend. The trail leads over a low saddle before paralleling the river and leading back to the water. It takes about 20 minutes to make the walk. In taking this trail, you will be bypassing the final gorge of the day—a sievey canyon cutting through Tapeats Sandstone.

The first two rapids of this Tapeats gorge are usually portaged due to rock and log strainers. The third drop has a run on the left at most water levels. One more class IV rapid and another sieve portage or two takes you out of the undercut-prone sandstone and back into the familiar gray bedrock, bringing two class IV's and a final class V.

Not far below here the canyon relents and you'll drift past the far end of the shortcut trail. From here, a mile or two of class II remains to the take-out below Doll Baby. Watch for fences and logs in this last stretch.

Logistics: A shuttle driver is highly recommended for the East Verde. Unless you live in Payson, it takes a painfully early start to drive the shuttle and make the run in the same day. The shuttle isn't terribly long, but the road is rough and often muddy when the East Verde is running.

The put-in is just northwest of Payson where Highway 87 crosses the river. Put in at the beach just downstream from the road crossing.

The take-out is downstream of Doll Baby Ranch where the road nears the river at a picnic/camping area. To get there, take Main Street off of Highway 87 in Payson. Main turns into forest road #406, also called LF Ranch Road. It is about 12 miles from Payson to the river.

Lower East Verde
(wilderness run)

This section of the East Verde runs through quintessential Arizona wilderness. The first few miles below Doll Baby Ranch are a braided, tree-cluttered mess, but just when things seem desperate, the river falls away into a beautiful class IV drop. For the next several miles, the river is primarily a pool-drop ribbon of class III and IV boulder gardens. There are still occasional tree-infested gravel bars, but the many clean drops overshadow the few inconveniences. It is 45 miles from Doll Baby to Horseshoe Dam on the Verde, making this at least an overnight trip. Combine it with the run above Doll Baby for a great 3-day run. The shuttle is 150 miles long.

Whitewater Rivers **191**

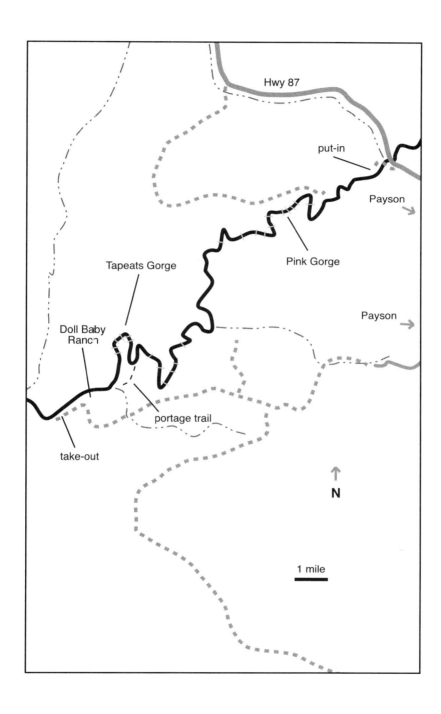

East Verde
(park & huck section)

Upstream from the Highway 87 bridge, the East Verde is mostly a tree-lined channel with little gradient. There is one short section of the creek, however, that cuts dramatically through granite bedrock (the same formation that forms the Pink Gorge downstream) in a series of steep rapids and waterfalls. To get here, take Houston Mesa Road for several miles out of Payson until the road crosses the river. The park & huck gorge is just upstream from this bridge. Continue up the road about another mile to the put-in.

This section of the East Verde is brief but memorable. The creek abruptly goes from a placid stream in the pines to a rocky class V—VI whitewater gorge. The entry rapid drops into a walled-in slot with a giant boulder sieve directly below. At low water, the sieve has a runnable tunnel on the right. At higher water, it is a death trap, forcing paddlers to find a difficult put-in just below. The next rapid is called Jedi Landing. May the force be with you in finding the narrow landing zone. Below this is a long sluice coined Birthday Slide, which leads down to a broad right corner where Ellison Creek enters from the left in dramatic fashion.

If the East Verde is too high, the confluence falls on Ellison Creek might offer satisfaction for those with big drop fever. The real crux of Confluence Falls lies in making a take-out eddy after dumping into the East Verde. At high water, there is little time before the river dumps over class VI Novocaine Falls.

This 20-footer drops into a canyon narrows of foamy aerated water. The painful sounding title was dubbed, as were all the rapids, by Roy Lippman and Harlan Taney who were the first to run it, at roughly 150 cfs. Shortly below, the gorge relents, but there are still a couple class III—IV rapids that lead down to the best take-out: a campsite on river right just above the bridge.

Ellison Creek

Cody Howard ran Ellison Creek during summer high water, putting in a quarter-mile upstream of the East Verde confluence at a private property boundary. His report follows. *There is a steep 40-foot sliding falls (very tricky) with an old growth in the base of it. It would be sweet at epic flood stage. Downstream there were low angle slides and small rapids leading to the confluence slide. Confluence Slide was cool, but the real treat on the creek is the upper falls.*

Whitewater Rivers 193

Checkin' the STOMP!

Christopher Creek

General Description: A short steep gorge with big waterfalls
Difficulty: V — V+
Gradient: 360 fpm
Length: 1 mile
Flow: minimum: 50 cfs
 ideal: 100 — 150 cfs
Gage: Tonto Creek above Gun Creek (This gage is 50 miles downstream. It will give you an idea of how the drainage is flowing, but the best gage is visual. If Tonto is over 200 cfs, Christopher is worth a look.
Shuttle: 1 mile hike
Elevation: 5,300'
Likely Season: February, March, April
Peak Flow: Tonto Creek's peak flow is 72,500 cfs January 8, 1993.
Extrapolating this flow to Christopher would equal roughly 10,000 cfs.

This tributary to upper Tonto Creek runs through an awesome bedrock gorge with a gradient of 360 fpm. The creek does not have a large drainage basin, but it is located just below the impressive wall of the Mogollon Rim, where storms tend to release the bulk of their moisture. Another factor in paddler's favor is the fact that the creek doesn't take much water to become runnable.

On the first attempted descent in 2005, our group of five launched with about 130 cfs. At a clean looking 13-foot waterfall a few hundred yards into the gorge, paddler Roy Lippman of Flagstaff hit a rock at the base of the drop, and severely broke his left ankle. A lengthy evacuation ensued, requiring three of us to assist Roy in his painful crawl out of the canyon. Back in Flag, he underwent five hours of leg surgery.

Kyle McCutchen, Evan Stafford, and Todd Gillman of Colorado came through a few weeks later during research for their guide *Whitewater of the Southern Rockies*. They were able to finish the run on an estimated 100 cfs, and reported only two portages. They called it "a definite elbow pad run," but were very stoked on the dramatic waterfalls and slot rapids they found, bestowing the Coen Brothers-honoring titles of Big Lebowski and Little Lebowski to the tallest drops. Ever since, Christopher Creek has garnered more attention than any other AZ creek, becoming a regular stop for class V paddlers in the region.

Since I recommend hiking your shuttle for this run, it might make sense to drop your boat(s) near the head of the gorge and scamper along the rim to get a preliminary scout of the canyon. Once on the water, an 8-foot ledge serves as entrance to the gorge, and several more steep drops into slow pools come in quick succession.

Whitewater Rivers 195

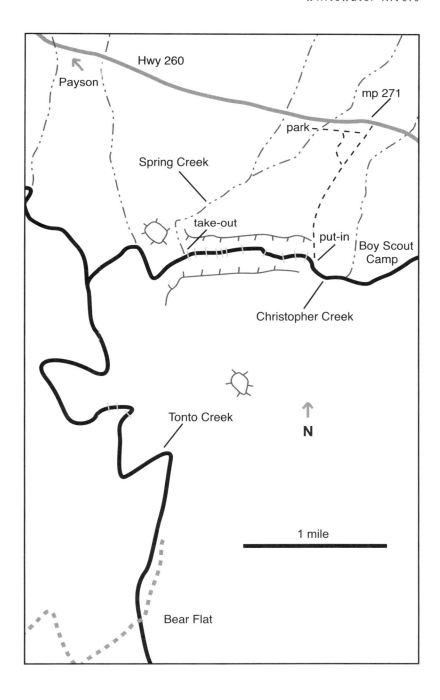

A couple hundred yards into the gorge, beware of a 13' vertical drop requiring a boof left. This is Roy's Smiles to Trials, named for the aforementioned leg break and evacuation. Below this are several slides, slots, and falls, culminating with a three-part series title Donnie's Drop (15'), Big Lebowski (30'), and Little Lebowski (20'). Portaging this crux section requires rope work and downclimbing, and escape from the canyon here would be steep, loose, and harrowing.

Downstream from the three big drops, there are a couple good rapids, and a couple more that are normally portaged. The streambed changes from rhyolite bedrock to boulders, the gorge begins to relent, and Spring Creek enters on river right. This is a good exit point unless you wish to continue downstream to Tonto Creek for a take-out at Bear Flat. See the Tonto Creek Headwaters description for details on that. Hiking out at Spring Creek generally takes about 30 minutes to reach your vehicle and/or Hwy 260. About 15 minutes' walk from Christopher Creek, there is a cairned route leading out the creek right bank of Spring Creek. Follow this, or find your own meandring route around the chaparral thickets in a northeasterly direction back to the highway.

Logistics: Park near milepost 270.7 off the east bound lanes, where a gated dirt road leads to an old quarry clearing. Hike east from here, generally paralleling the highway on an old railroad grade. In about 0.3 miles from the parking spot, after crossing a fence, intersect social trails that lead south toward the gorge from the old milepost 271 access (now closed). There is a cairned shortcut route that heads into the woods earlier if you're feeling bold. In any case, continue south / southeast toward the sound of whitewater, and you will arrive at the rim of the gorge. Head upstream, where a network of social trails will lead to the creek at the head of the canyon.

Roy's Smiles to Trials

Tonto Creek
(Hellsgate)

General Description: A classic wilderness run through scenic gorges
Difficulty: IV — V
Gradient: 89 fpm through gorge / steepest mile 160 fpm
Length: 26 miles (a long 2 or easy 3 days)
Flow: minimum: 500 cfs on gage (sometimes less if the water is coming from high in the basin)
      ideal: 700 — 1,000 cfs on gage
Gage: Tonto Creek above Gun Creek
Shuttle: About 36 miles, mostly pavement and good dirt road, but with a couple creek crossings
Elevation: 4,900'—2,900'
Likely Season: late February, March, April
Peak Flow: 72,500 cfs January 8, 1993.

In *The Best Whitewater in California,* author Chuck Stanley says, "This is it! The Middle Fork of the Feather is the best self-supported wilderness trip in California." This quote comes to mind when I think of the Hellsgate run on Tonto Creek. This is the Middle Feather of Arizona. The scenery is fantastic, the camping is good, the low elevation climate is moderate, and the whitewater is good "easy" class V.

The creek at the Bear Flat put-in might look paltry, but numerous small side creeks boost the flow as you travel downstream, growing Tonto into a decent stream. If there is 100 cfs at the put-in, you'll usually have plenty of water.

    Even on this small flow, nice rapids start right away as the creek enters a canyon of hard red rock. Bony boulder gardens and occasional bedrock flumes alternate throughout the first several miles. Although the creek leads through a few different narrow canyons in its first miles, the most notable gorge on the first part of the run is Hellsgate, about eight miles below the put-in.

Hellsgate is an ominous dark cleft containing three major rapids. The first features a sticky hole and an undercut cliff. Fortunately, there is a portage route. The next rapid would be very difficult or impossible to portage. Fortunately, it is runnable. The last drop in Hellsgate is a nice simple boof. Soon after this you will emerge into welcome light where Haigler Creek comes in from the left.

Haigler nearly doubles the flow, the creek mellows for a couple miles, and the canyon deepens. The first gorge below Haigler is short and sievey with easy portaging if necessary. After a mile or two with a couple class III's, the canyon suddenly pinches into The Mouse Trap. This boulder sieve jammed in a narrows is a seemingly nightmarish spot, but there is a bank to get out on just above it, and with a little climbing a good scout is possi-

Whitewater Rivers 199

Harlan Taney exits Last Hurrah Gorge

ble. The sieve usually turns out to be runnable anyway.

Another open section of read & run class III and IV leads to Black Flush, a two drop series pinched between smooth black walls. Following this adrenaline pumper, there is more mellow water and open country through Derrick Pocket. After Spring Creek enters, the creek makes a hard left into a dramatic sheer-walled gorge of class III. Another relatively open section follows before yet one more ominous gorge pinches in.

This one contains a couple class IV's and V's, all of which are portageable. Emerging from this canyon, a new scene of saguaro cactus and bright orange California poppies will welcome you to the desert near the confluence of Green Valley Creek.

The river weaves through huge pink hippopotamus rocks before the whitewater gradually builds to a climax in Last Hurrah Gorge. A class V rapid leads into the gorge, then comes a class VI drop with a thin portage route on the left. The last rapid just above the mouth of the gorge is a steep blind class V requiring some careful team rope work to scout or portage. Negotiating this last big drop is a fitting final challenge to an epic trip. High water would probably necessitate a portage of the entire Last Hurrah Gorge.

You are through the gnar, but don't let your guard down too much, because a couple class IV rapids remain as the creek tumbles out into the Gisela Valley. After this you'll still have a few long miles of winding through river cane and willows before reaching the take-out at the boat beach below Gisela.

Logistics: The take-out is at the boat beach (sometimes called Cottonwood Beach) in Gisela. This is at the downstream edge of the community. It's the standard creek access in town. Ask a local. The turn off Highway 87 to Gisela is 10.6 miles south of Mazatzal Casino in Payson.

The put-in is Bear Flat. Take Highway 260 east out of Payson for about 13 miles and turn onto the signed dirt road leading to Bear Flat. It is about 5 miles from the highway to Bear Flat. You will have to cross Thompson Draw a few times en route. If crossing this little creek is too difficult for a small truck, Tonto Creek is probably too high to run anyway.

Whitewater Rivers 201

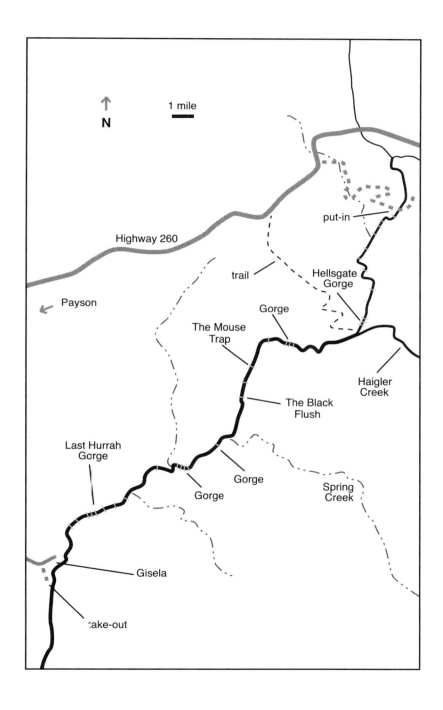

Tonto Creek

Lower Gorge
(Rye Creek to Gun Creek)

General Description: A scenic desert run in a canyon
Difficulty: III
Gradient: 38 fpm/steepest mile—50 fpm
Length: 5 miles
Flow: minimum: 300 cfs
  ideal: 600 — 1,000 cfs
Gage: Tonto Creek at Gun Creek
Shuttle: 6.5 miles, pavement and good dirt roads, bikeable
Elevation: 2,700'—2,500'
Likely Season: February—April
Peak Flow: 72,500 cfs January 8, 1993.

Okay, here it is, that one glaring entry I have in each of my guidebooks that makes me cringe with guilt. Tonto Creek is a sensitive place, and has potential for overuse. I'd love to keep it a secret. Tonto is a standard AZ whitewater run close to Phoenix—a class III classic. To exclude it from this guide would be like ignoring the elephant in the room. Please be especially aware and respectful when visiting Tonto. It's a cool place, and hopefully it will stay that way.

A Tonto run starts with a run on tiny Rye Creek. This will usually be running about 30 cfs when Tonto is up. At this level, it takes about 10 minutes of paddling on Rye to reach Tonto. Rye Creek is a brush fest at first, then a little bedrock section begins that actually makes 30 cfs seem reasonable. Just before reaching Tonto, watch for a fence across Rye Creek which can usually be avoided without too much problem. There is a ranch house near here. Proceed quickly and quietly.

Just below the confluence of Rye and Tonto Creeks, there is a ledgy class III—Rye Creek Rapid. This is where trouble began for Wes Hall in 1993 when he and his partner attempted the run at 20,000 cfs, certainly a class V level. A swim and flush drowning ensued. There is a memorial plaque for Wes on the rim of the canyon downstream, near a hidden and spectacular side creek.

Below Rye Creek Rapids, the river bounces along between hillsides of juniper and saguaro and dynamically patterned rocky bluffs. Small beaches tuck beneath cliffs of pink, black, white, and rose-colored rocks. The whitewater remains mostly class II for a couple miles until a gorge forms, bringing the whitewater up a notch in difficulty.

The Gauntlet is the first rapid of the canyon. Here a fin of rock splits the river. A small channel goes right, while most of the water stays left, feeding into a formidable but runnable hole. Below this the river's pace is swifter as it races through the gorge with occasional class III rapids. There

Whitewater Rivers 203

Lisa Gelzis

Tonto Creek—an Arizona classic

is one spot where the canyon pinches to a narrow 12-foot passage. Fortunately, the gradient has slackened at this point, making for an intimidating yet relatively non-threatening scene.

Over a mile of scenic canyon with class I and II ushers you out to the mouth of the gorge. After passing the gage, you'll run a class II, cross a pool, and shoot one more riffle before taking out on the right in a long straightaway bordered by gravel.

Logistics: A creekside take-out is reachable for 4WD vehicles, while less sturdy vehicles will have to park a couple hundred yards uphill from the creek. To reach the take-out area, take Highway 188 south past Jakes Corner for 2.7 miles and turn east onto a dirt road. Follow this road about 0.5 miles back north, and if your rig can make it, down the hill to the riverbed.

The put-in is reached by traveling back to Jakes Corner and turning east onto dirt road #184. Follow #184 about 2.7 miles to a spur road located just up the hill from the #184 bridge over Rye Creek. This spur road leads a hundred yards or so to an abandoned closed road that provides a short walk down to the creek.

If road #184 between Jakes Corner and Rye Creek is closed or impassable, you can reach the Rye Creek bridge by traveling in on #184 from the other direction. Drive out to Highway 87, north for 3.8 miles to the Gisela turn, east for 0.1 miles to road #184, and south on #184 for 4.7 miles to the bridge.

In the past, river runners have put-in at Gisela, several miles upstream from Rye Creek. This is not recommended, however. Between Gisela and Rye Creek, there is very little whitewater, a few fences across the river, and a sensitive bald eagle nesting zone.

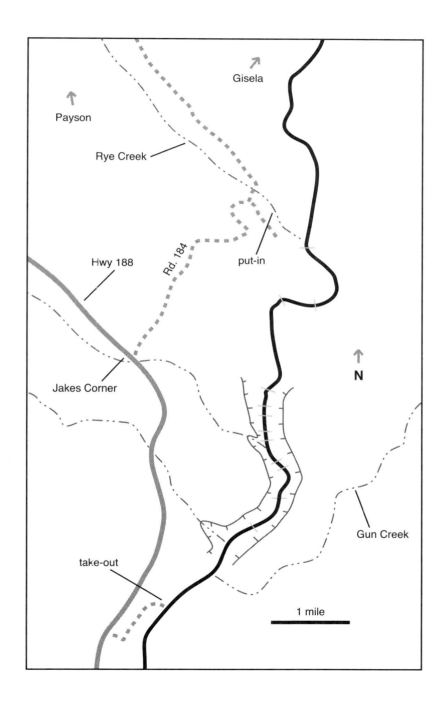

Tonto Creek
(Headwaters run)

When Tonto Creek is raging at several thousand cfs or more in its lower reaches, the upper forks of the creek above Bear Flat can be run. I haven't done this section, but Jim McComb led a team down it during a flood day in the winter of 2005.

They put-in at the fish hatchery just beneath the Mogollon Rim. Despite being very near the stream's source, they had an estimated 300 cfs on this high water day. The first couple miles were a mostly eddy-less sluice. McComb reports one 9-foot ledge in the first miles above the Highway 260 bridge. There must be some other exciting spots too, because one member of the party had an entertaining hole ride and decided to call it a day at the highway bridge.

The remainder of the group found themselves on 1,000 cfs by the time they reached Christopher Creek. Not far below the confluence of Christopher, Tonto Creek enters a gorge. At high water, there are some sizeable class V's in here, but a high portage route avoids the worst of it. At moderate levels, it is pool / drop class IV.

At Bear Flat, the creek was a robust 2,000 cfs or more, and each low-water road crossing was a huge hole. The other complication of doing this run is driving into Bear Flat. Crossing Thompson Draw en-route can be difficult or impossible during periods of very high water.

Tonto Creek whitewater

Salome Creek

Salome Creek cuts through spectacular granite gorges as it runs south out of the Sierra Ancha Range. The lower reaches of the creek flows through the Salome Jug, a narrow cleft in the Sonoran Desert. The Jug has been a renowned canyoneering destination for some time (see *Canyoneering Arizona*), but Cody Howard has now brought kayaking to the mix here.

The creek is very constricted, with limited eddies above a normally portaged 30' waterfall near the end of the gorge, so a thorough scout of the canyon is recommended before paddling. Polished granite in the upper part of the Jug creates beatiful slides and falls, and the scenery is outrageous. If you care to enter this realm of canyoneraking, aim for a water level that's b g enough to float a boat, but not much more. Ideal flows are 15 to 30 cfs. If the adjacent gaged drainage, Cherry Creek, is running between 20 and 50 cfs, the Jug might be worth a look. Take Highway 188 south from Highway 87 to near milepost 255, about 8 miles south of Punkin Center. Follow A Cross Road #60 east for 10 miles and park at the Jug trailhead. It is an easy 2-mile walk to the head of the gorge.

The upper gorges of Salome also saw kayak travel at the hands of Cody Howard. Here the creek drops up to 400 fpm through more extensive granite gorges. Logistics are difficult, with long muddy roads and capricious water levels. In the gorges, low water levels are a must. Below the gorges, high water is a must, and at that point you are at least a several mile hike from anywhere. The one descent was aborted, but was reportedly rife with physical effort and high adventure, if not quality paddling.

Salt River
(Upper-Daily)

General Description: The most popular daily whitewater run in Arizona, with fun rapids in a beautiful canyon
Difficulty: III — III+ (IV)
Gradient: 35 fpm
Length: 6 to 8 miles
Flow: minimum: 500 cfs for rafts, 300 cfs for kayaks, 200 cfs for inflatable kayaks
    ideal: 1,000 — 3,000 cfs
Gage: Salt near Chrysotile
Shuttle: 4 to 6 miles, bikeable
Elevation: 3,400'—3,100'
Likely Season: February—early May / Heavy monsoon years provide flows in August and September.
Peak Flow: Chrysotile gage—76,600 cfs January 8, 1993.
Permits: Permits are required from the Apache Tribe. Details are below. Call 928-338-4385 for more information.

Ask most paddlers throughout the Western U.S. to name a river in Arizona besides the Colorado in Grand Canyon, and they will quickly answer "the Salt." This is the most widely-known whitewater day run in the state, and dedicated paddlers have long been flocking here for early spring boating. There is a commercial rafting scene here as well, making it the first stop on the circuit for full-time river guides.

These boatmen will tell you the first thing you need to know about the Salt is that it is on Apache land. A daily fee is charged ($15 per person per day in 2010) to run the river, and permits are checked. During the season, you can usually purchase permits at the Salt River Canyon Store on Highway 60. Permits are also sometimes available from K-mart in Show Low, or the Carrizo Junction Store twenty miles north of the river on Highway 60. Contact the Apache Tribe at 928-338-4385 for more information.

The standard put-in is located at a large eddy a few hundred yards down the road from the highway. Some elect to launch closer to the highway bridge, however, and run a gravel bar rapid above the main put-in.

There is another short steep gravel bar leading into a wall immediately below the main put-in eddy, then a long straight-away leads to Tailings Rapid, where the river bends right. Next is Bump & Grind—an aptly named shallow gravel bar. The narrow rapid just below here that sluices against the right wall is called Maytag. This one tends to spin rafts around, hence the name. It is fast and powerful, but straightforward with no big holes. Next is Grumman, where some sizeable holes do lurk. The river makes a sharp right along a cliff wall above Mother Rock. At higher flows,

Whitewater Rivers 209

A rafting party enjoys the Salt

look for a great surf hole above Mother Rock on the right. Next is Eagles Nest, sometimes called Overboard. This is a left turn with some big potentially hazardous rocks along the right bank. At most levels, a good play hole exists toward the bottom of the rapid. This same hole can of course flip small rafts or unsuspecting paddlers.

Some class II water below Eagles Nest is the end of the Mule Hoof Bend section of rapids. If there were a trail, one could hike up to the road from here, and then walk a short quarter-mile back to the put-in. For now, this shortcut route is a difficult desert bushwhack that is rarely attempted.

The next few miles of river are splashy class I and II. Just past 2nd Campground where raft guides and other paddlers often camp, the river bends right into Exhibition Rapid. This one holds the biggest waves on the run. A few easy ledge rapids lead down to Cibecue Rapid and Cibecue Creek, a popular take-out.

For those who continue downstream, a steep gravel bar called 3-way keeps the action going, then the river turns right into Salt River Draw Rapid. Next is Mescal, a simple yet forceful drop with a fast and shallow hole. Just below Mescal is the last good place to take out, because the road climbs away from the river after this. Also, the Salt Banks are just downstream on river right. This is a sacred Apache site, and strictly off-limits.

Logistics: The dirt road on river right serves as access for this run. It is rocky and narrow, but passable to two-wheel drives down to Cibecue Creek. Getting across Cibecue often requires four-wheel-drive and/or high clearance. It is completely impassable when the creek is high.

There are some small parking spots near Cibecue Creek, and just upstream. If you continue downstream to below Mescal Rapid, there are plenty of parking options there too.

It is 4 miles from the put-in to Cibecue Creek, and another couple miles to the take-outs below Mescal.

Whitewater Rivers 211

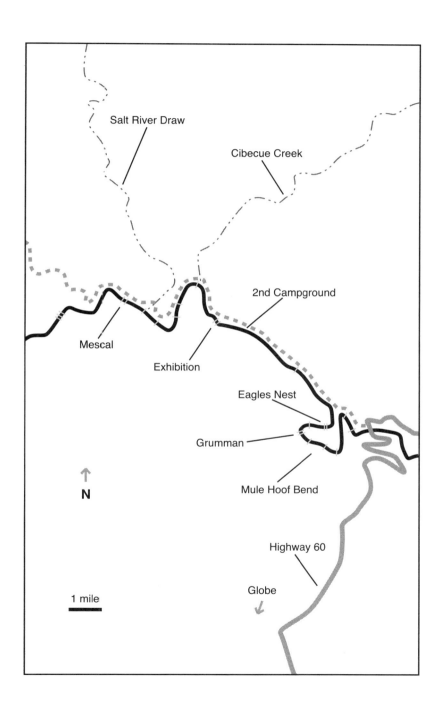

Salt River
(wilderness)

General Description: A three to five-day run down a classic river in the Sonoran Desert
Difficulty: III—IV
Gradient: 22 fpm
Length: 52 miles (including day stretch)
Flow: minimum: 400 cfs (many runs have been made at lower levels)
ideal: 1,000 — 3,000 cfs
Gage: Salt River near Chrysotile is the put-in gage. Salt River near Roosevelt is the take-out gage.
Shuttle: 64 miles, paved
Elevation: 3,400'—2,200'
Likely Season: March—May
Peak Flow: Chrysotile gage—76,600 cfs January 8, 1993. Roosevelt gage—143,000 cfs January 8, 1993.
Permits: Permits are required for the wilderness section from March 1— May 15. Call the Tonto National Forest (928-402-6200) for more information. Permits from the Apache Tribe are required for the upper section. See the Salt River (upper-daily) description on the previous pages for details.

A multi-day on the Salt is the classic Arizona river trip. Great scenery, good hiking, fun rapids, and the surreal juxtaposition of saguaro cactus next to a burgeoning river makes this a must-do trip for dedicated river runners.

Most trips put-in at the Highway 60 bridge. For more detail on these first several miles below the bridge, consult the Salt Daily description in this book.

Once below Ledges Rapid 10 miles downstream of the put-in, you're not likely to see any more of the day paddlers, and a wilderness feel sets in. If you have made it through the rapids of the day stretch, nothing in the next several miles should be of any special concern. White Rock Rapid, however, does come up quickly as the river makes a 90 degree right turn 14 miles down.

As the rapid title implies, the river enters beautiful white granite in this section, narrowing into a low canyon before the confluence of Canyon Creek. The water is swift in here, and you might zoom right by this dramatic side creek if you aren't attentive. Not far below Canyon Creek, the terrain opens at Gleason Flat. There are roads on both sides of the river here. Both roads are long and rough, but they do offer access in a pinch.

Below Gleason the Salt River Canyon Wilderness officially begins on river left, while river right remains the White Mountain Apache Reservation until Lower Corral Canyon, located several miles farther downstream.

Whitewater Rivers 213

The Salt winds through Jump Off Canyon

Within a couple miles below Gleason Flat, you'll encounter Eye of the Needle Rapid, and Black Rock—a class IV drop.

Class II and III action continues for several miles as the river winds through desert hills. The whitewater picks up and the canyon pinches down below Lower Corral Canyon. First is The Maze, and then Pinball. Both of these bouldery rapids require ferry moves in swift current. The scenery gets more dramatic below here as the river enters Jump Off Canyon. Steep fins of Quartzite knife into the river, one of which forms Quartzite Falls.

Quartzite Falls was once a formidable drop containing a very sticky hole, and most trips portaged. In 1993, a misguided engineer who also happened to be a weekend raft guide hiked in and blew up the hydraulic-forming ledge. The once magnificent and powerful rapid is now emasculated to a shadow of its former self. On the brighter side, it is still a solid class IV drop, and the jackass who blew it up with his friends did indeed do some time in the big house.

Just below Quartzite, Corkscrew Rapid is the final major obstacle in Jump Off Canyon. The river remains swift with occasional class III down to Cherry Creek, then you are officially on the paddle out.

This final 16 miles contains nice scenery, some great volleyball/horseshoes beaches, and wildlife. I was lucky enough to see a mountain lion down here once—a special treat on any river, much less one that runs through saguaro country.

Logistics: The take-out is near the bridge over the Salt on Highway 288 north of Globe. This is a few miles before the Salt runs into Roosevelt Reservoir. There is a gravel parking area for boaters nearby, and a concrete ramp at the river.

To reach the put-in, return to Globe, then proceed north on Highway 60. The put-in is just downstream of the Highway 60 bridge in Salt River Canyon. This is on Apache land, and there is a $15 per person per day permit required. Call 928-338-4385 for information on where to obtain Apache permits. Call 928-402-6200 for information on wilderness permits from the Tonto National Forest, or visit www.fs.fed.us/r3/tonto/home.shtml

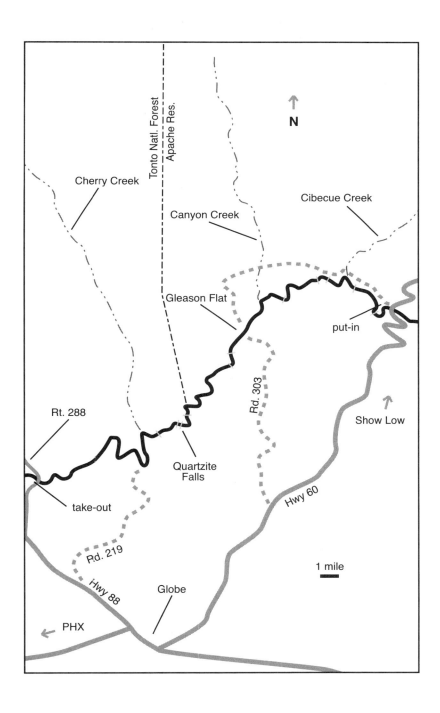

Upper Black River

General Description: A small mountain river in beautiful wild country
Difficulty: III (IV)
Gradient: 58 fpm / steepest mile 100 fpm
Length: 12 miles
Flow: minimum: 75 cfs at put-in, 150 cfs at take-out
ideal: 300 cfs at put-in, 700 cfs at take-out
Gage: Black River near Point of Pines. You will have 50% to 75% of this flow, so an ideal flow for this run would usually be a reading of about 900 to 1,200 cfs on the Point of Pines gage.
Shuttle: 13 miles, good dirt road that can be snowed-in early in the season. Call the forest service in Alpine for current conditions: 928-339-4384.
Elevation: 7,500' — 6,800'
Likely Season: March, April
Peak Flow: Point of Pines gage—17,900 cfs, October 19, 1972.

The Black River is the main source of the Salt River. The Black runs for roughly 100 miles before its confluence with the White River forms the Salt. Most of the Black runs through the Apache Reservation, and as of 2007 it is still off-limits to boating. The section described here, however, is located on national forest land upstream of the reservation.

The put-in is actually on the East Fork of the Black, about a half mile upstream from the confluence of the West Fork, where the main Black begins. The East Fork usually carries 25% more flow than the West Fork, so it is the preferred put-in location.

Class III rapids begin shortly below the confluence. Most of the drops are basalt boulder gardens with at least one nasty pin rock lurking. At low water, the rapids are technical and shallow. At higher water, they develop fast lead-ins with scarce eddies. This is a swift mountain river, and slowing down to look for hazards can sometimes be difficult. Get your willow-grabbing skills ready! There is one class IV on the run—a short steep boulder-choked affair.

About a third of the way through the run, the rapids begin to slacken and the wildlife watching picks up. Ospreys make their nests in ponderosa pines, and bighorn sheep stand on rocky outcrops. Elk, deer, turkeys, and coyotes are commonly spotted. The dense spruce and fir forests of the north-facing slopes make good bear habitat. Perhaps the most exciting wildlife spotting would be that of a Mexican Grey Wolf. Several packs now roam the area.

Logistics: Take Highway 191 between Hannagan Meadow and Alpine, and turn onto forest road #26. This leads several miles to road #24, which heads north a couple of miles to the put-in on the East Fork near Buffalo Crossing.

For the take-out, continue across the river and take road #25 about a dozen miles to Wildcat Crossing.

Whitewater Rivers 217

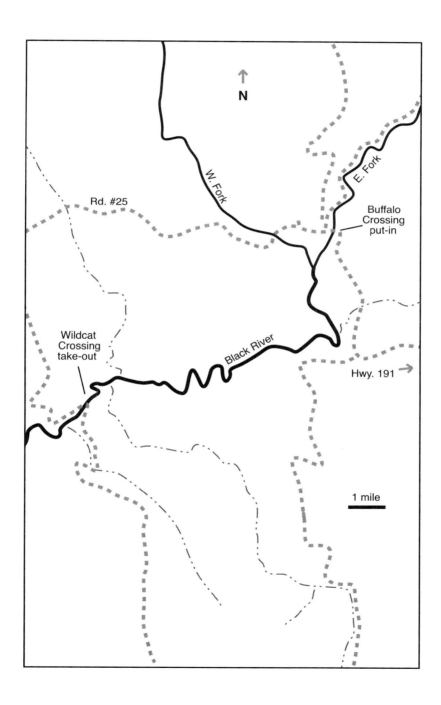

Upper Little Colorado

General Description: A short steep creek run
Difficulty: V
Gradient: 0.5 miles at 40, 180, 250
Length: 2.5 miles
Flow: minimum: 120 cfs
ideal: 200 — 250 cfs
Gage: Little Colorado River above Lyman Lake
Shuttle: 7 miles, bikeable
Elevation: 6,630 — 6,180
Likely Season: April
Peak Flow: 16,000 cfs July 25, 1940

The upper Little Colorado bears little resemblance to the warm turquoise lower Little Colorado most of us know in Grand Canyon. By contrast, the upper LCR is a snow fed creek draining the northern slopes of the White Mountains. In fact, the waters of the upper LCR don't even make it to the dramatic Little Colorado Gorge downstream. When Lyman Lake Reservoir doesn't stop all the upper LCR's water, thirsty desert sands do.

Before this modest mountain stream gets swallowed by the Painted Desert, it tumbles through a basalt canyon beneath the wind-swept plains of eastern Arizona. Within the basalt canyon, the creek is constricted and steep, creating good whitewater.

Before reaching the rapids, you will have to negotiate a few fences. The fences are there, of course, to manage the flourishing bovine population that grazes near the creek. Unless you are immune to Giardia, keep your mouth closed tightly on this run.

The cow country float changes dramatically when the fences are replaced by technical boulder gardens. At flows over 200 cfs there are clean lines through most of the rapids, but using the rocks of the riverbed is always standard technique on this small creek. The tight slots require precise boat control, and the angular rocks constantly make unexpected grabs for your paddle.

During our first time down this run, Lisa's borrowed paddle was lost in a wipe-out, forcing a hike to the take-out. Returning a week later, my paddle snapped in two on a Duffek stroke! This time, I was the one hiking to the take-out. A spare paddle is not a bad idea on the upper LCR.

If all goes well, you will enjoy a lively two miles of whitewater. The drops are steep, and the pools are short. All rapids are formed by medium-sized basalt boulders. There is one memorable class V+ that is usually portaged. It is a long rapid that spills over two clean chutes before splitting into two channels—one flows into an overhanging juniper, and the other terminates in a row of boulders. The portage is an easy over-the-fence affair on the left.

Whitewater Rivers 219

High plains creekin'

The last quarter mile of the run eases as the pools get longer. The take-out is located where the canyon relents to a bucolic valley. This is state land, but private property is nearby, so be low-key and stay clear of the ranch homes.

Logistics: To reach the take-out, turn east onto road #4162 from Highway 180. This is about 15 miles north of St. Johns, between mp 386 and 387. A couple hundred yards from the highway, turn right onto road #4005. Stay right at the fork in a mile, and proceed another 0.4 miles to the gate indicating state trust land. A permit to use state land can be obtained from the state land department 520-367-0313.

For the put-in, return to the highway and head south for 3.8 miles, turning east on a dirt road 0.2 miles past mp 390. This dirt road leads 1.5 miles to the rim of the canyon where a trail leads about 200 yards down to the creek.

Upper LCR—the paddle buster

Whitewater Rivers 221

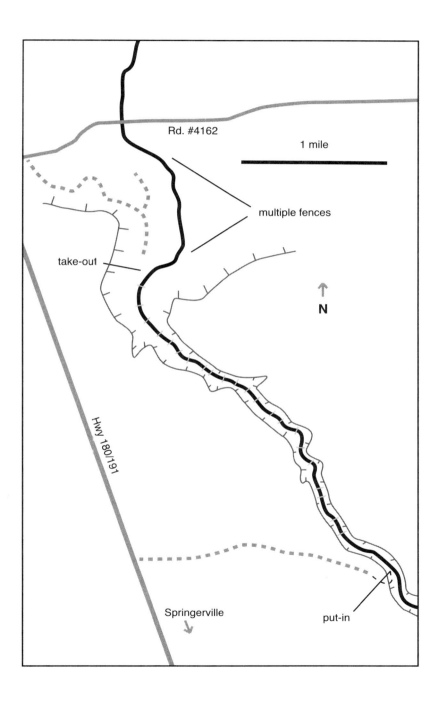

East Clear Creek

East Clear Creek drains a large part of the Mogollon Rim. Its headwaters tap aspen-lined meadows at 7,500 feet. Several of these high feeder creeks get impounded in Blue Ridge Reservoir at the 6,700-foot elevation. In dry years, the reservoir won't even fill up, and therefore no water will spill over into the creek downstream. In wet years when the reservoir is spilling, the creek can run quite high, and is a major source of the Little Colorado River.

There are a few significant tributary creeks that enter below the reservoir. In marginal water years, these can sometimes produce enough water to run the lower reaches of the creek even if Blue Ridge isn't spilling. Access to the sheer canyon is difficult. I've spent entire days driving dirt roads in the surrounding ranch country trying to find the river, and failed. Good luck.

Glenn Rink, Josh Lowry, and the late John Foss explored East Clear in the early '90s. They put-in near East Sunset Mountain and paddled the 40 miles or so down to McHood Lake near Winslow. Whenever I asked Rink about the trip, his recollections were vague except that Foss was disappointed that there wasn't more whitewater on the run. Given this information, an East Clear descent never made the top of my to-do list.

I finally ran East Clear during March of 2005 with Matt Fayhee and Jesse Perry. Now I consider it a standard Arizona multi-day. I've yet to put in at Blue Ridge Reservoir, but a Mack's Crossing put-in works just fine. This is off of Highway 87 at the back of a housing development, 13 miles below the reservoir, and 60 miles above McHood Lake. The road to the creek is 4 WD. It is an easy 1-mile downhill walk to the water from near the top of the canyon.

There are gages on East Clear, both at the upstream and downstream reservoirs, that come in and out of service. If neither cfs gage is working, the Blue Ridge Reservoir level might still offer an indication of flow. If it is over 100 percent of capacity, the creek is running. At 101 percent capacity, you will have roughly 400 cfs at Mack's Crossing. This translates to nearly 1,000 cfs by the take-out at McHood Reservoir near Winslow—a good level.

It takes 4 days to paddle the seemingly endless canyon of Coconino Sandstone and Kaibab Limestone. At the put-in, the slopes of the canyon are covered in Douglas firs and pines; by the take-out only cactus cling to the rocky walls. Within the remote canyon there is profligate wildlife, including many raptors. There is also rock art and ruins.

The whitewater consists of mostly class II up high, with occasional III's. Farther downstream, there are several juicy class III rapids, and plenty of brush. There are two bad sieves on the run. One is a runnable class V with bad consequences, the other is a total sieve with the entire river going under big rocks. Most of the good class III and IV rapids are sievey in nature too, so be cautious. There are four to six class IV drops on the run, most of which are located toward the lower end. The grand finale is a class IV pinched between vertical walls of sandstone. At 1,000 cfs, there is no scouting or portaging this one!

Chevelon Creek

Chevelon Creek parallels East Clear Creek, running from the Mogollon Rim north to the Little Colorado River. In its upper reaches, the creek flows through pine and fir forests between two impoundments—Woods Canyon Lake and Chevelon Canyon Lake. Not far below Chevelon Canyon Lake is Chevelon Crossing, the highest upstream anyone has put in.

From Chevelon Crossing to for thirty-five miles downstream, the creek is brushy with class II and a couple III rapids. Petroglyphs are a highlight, and the canyon scenery is good. This section makes a nice three day trip. It is quite a thrill to hike out of the narrow slot and emerge on a huge wind swept plain, which is what surrounds this hidden gorge.

About 35 miles below Chevelon Crossing there a couple obscure private property put-ins for the Gods Pocket section, a class IV (V) run in a pretty sandstone canyon. Access changes annually, and it is never a simple affair.

Below the Gods Pocket section is the lower Chevelon run, a class II (III-) run with bizarre yet fairly non-threatening logjams in a narrow gorge, with awesome petroglyphs.

The best put-in for the lower run is on the property of Rock Art Canyon Ranch. Give them a call (928-288-3260) before your trip to get permission and put-in directions. The take-out is just below the McLaws Road bridge that crosses Chevelon Gorge.

San Francisco River

General Description: A scenic and mellow trip in remote wilderness
Difficulty: II (III)
Gradient: 18 fpm
Length: 62 miles—two to four days
Flow: minimum: 200 cfs at take-out
ideal: 500 cfs at take-out
Gage: San Francisco River at Clifton. There is also a gage near the put-in at Glenwood, NM.
Shuttle: 55 miles mostly on pavement
Elevation: 4,600'—3,500'
Likely Season: Late March through April or August and September
Peak Flow: 27,500 cfs October 2, 1983 near Glenwood / 90,900 cfs October 2, 1983 at Clifton

The San Francisco River runs through some of the most remote country in the Southwest. The Blue Range Primitive Area lies to the north of the river, while a de-facto wilderness of undeveloped ranchland is to the south. This is the domain of lions, bobcats, and bears. Re-introduced wolves were released north of here in 1998 with the intention that they would roam this area. However, a few territorial ranchers have had moderate success in thwarting these efforts. The wolves have been slow to get a foothold. This rancher-versus-wolf drama tells much about the region. Man has not yet tamed the wilderness here, and predators are still viewed as a threat.

The best way to penetrate this wild land is with a float trip down the San Francisco. The river will carry you with ease through the difficult and rugged countryside. Allow at least three or four days for the trip if you can.

You might even want to spend some time near the put-in soaking at Sundial Springs. It is a privately-owned hot spring and campground with tubs overlooking the river. Call ahead for reservations (505-539-2712).

Below Sundial Springs, the river enters a canyon, and views of the river's headwaters (the Mogollon Mountains) are replaced with cliffs of raw basalt. The riverbed is channelized enough to keep you moving along swiftly, demanding a wary eye for strainers. As with the entire San Francisco River, this initial canyon is filled with a prolific growth of willows, sycamores, and some of the most impressive Fremont cottonwoods you are likely to ever see.

As the basalt canyon broadens several miles below the put-in, small side creeks periodically enter the river and boost the flow. Though you might be able to keep track of your progress by noting these side creeks, the stream meanders radically for its entire length, making navigation difficult. The first good landmark comes about 25 miles into the run when powerlines cross the canyon at the Arizona/New Mexico border.

Beneath the powerlines is a wall-shot rapid with some funky currents. This rapid might be exciting, but it is less of a hazard than the strainers that poten-

San Francisco River

tially lurk around every bend. The other memorable rapid on the San Francisco is a diversion dam that could get nasty at high water. This is located near a ranch a few miles upstream from the confluence with the Blue River.

The Blue enters the San Francisco on river right about 20 miles upstream from Clifton. When mining roads begin to appear on the hillsides, you still have several miles to go before reaching the take-out in Clifton. This final stretch runs through some dramatic rocky mountains, but the wild feel of the upper river is gone.

The take-out at the highway bridge in Clifton is just down the street from Sanitary Market—an apparently clean place to get chips and beer.

Logistics: The take-out is at the highway bridge in Clifton, AZ. You can't miss it.

To reach the put-in, drive Highway 78 into New Mexico, then north on Highway 180 for 10.5 miles to road #519. Turn left onto #519 and make your way toward the river. Public river access in the area changes periodically. You might be able to pay for safe and convenient parking at Sundial Springs (505-539-2712).

Shuttle possibilities are Rusty in Cliff, NM (505-535-2905), or Richard McClusky, notable local laundarymat owner in Clifton, AZ.

Blue River

The Blue River drains the eastern slope of the White Mountains near the New Mexico state line. Starting amidst spruce-lined meadows, the small river slowly gains strength from a myriad of tributaries as it runs through the Blue Range Primitive Area, one of the wildest ecosystems in the Southwest. The Blue enters the San Francisco River about 17 miles upstream from the town of Clifton, so a run on the Blue ends with a paddle down the San Francisco. See the San Francisco River description for details on that river.

The most commonly used put-in is off Juan Miller Road #475. This dirt road leaves Highway 191 about 25 miles north of Clifton, and a couple miles past Upper Eagle Creek Road. It is about 15 miles down Juan Miller Road to the river. Launching here can provide a long one day trip down to Clifton, or an easy two day float.

I have never run the Blue, but reports are that it is mostly class II with a couple slightly harder rapids. The scenery is supposedly good. The surroundings are undeniably wild.

The river rarely gets higher than 200 cfs. This is probably a minimum flow. Your best chances of catching it with water are in late March or April following an above average winter. It occasionally runs in summer monsoon season also.

Whitewater Rivers 227

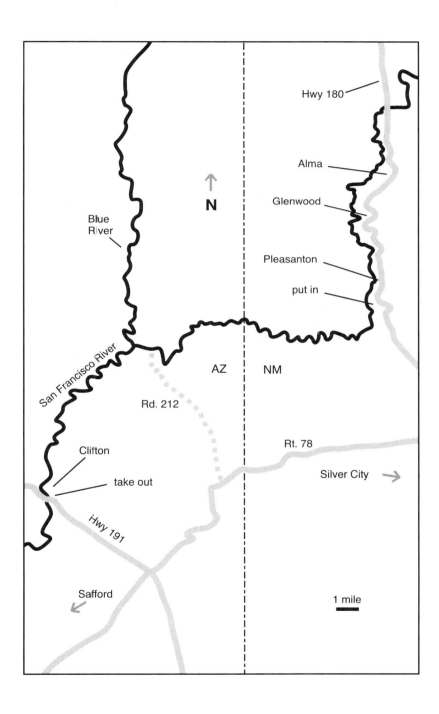

Gila Box
(San Francisco River to Safford)

General Description: A long one-day or easy two-day run in wild surroundings
Difficulty: II
Gradient: 11 fpm
Length: 20 miles if putting in on the Gila / 24.5 miles if launching on the San Francisco
Flow: minimum: 300 cfs
ideal: 700 — 2,000 cfs
Gage: Gila River at head of Safford Valley / There are also gages on the San Francisco and farther upstream on the Gila that can be helpful in assessing flows.
Shuttle: 34 miles, mostly paved, some graded dirt
Elevation: 3,360'—3,140' (San Francisco put-in is 4,040')
Likely Season: February—April, August—early September
Peak Flow: 132,000 cfs October 2, 1983

"Gila Box" is an frequently used term, referring to multiple stretches of the Gila depending on who you talk to. Most commonly, boaters call two different sections of the Gila "the box." One is a class III-IV run near the town of Redrock, New Mexico, where the river runs around the Big Burro Mountains. The other section is the one highlighted here. The river is class II, and in Arizona. Paddlers sometimes call it the Arizona Gila Box.

There are two commonly used put-ins for this run: the San Francisco River in Clifton, and the old highway bridge on the Gila. Launching directly on the Gila offers a somewhat shorter shuttle, and sometimes better flows, as the San Francisco River might not always be boatable when the Gila is running. Often, though, if the Gila is up, so is the San Francisco, and launching right in the town of Clifton is easy and unique. Additionally, there is a scenic canyon on the San Francisco just before it enters the Gila, and running two rivers on the same trip is always a bonus.

Wherever you decide to put-in, the river will be at its most narrow and challenging in the first miles. After the confluence of the Gila and San Francisco, the riverbed opens. Even though the river is not as tight below the confluence, pretty walls adorn most of the journey, and green riparian zones crowd the Gila's floodplains. Black hawks, peregrine falcons, and eagles are commonly spotted.

The whitewater is scattered and mellow. There are certainly enough rapids to keep novice boaters on their toes, and advanced river runners will find mild entertainment if they pursue it, but generally this is a scenic float. Campsites in the canyon aren't great, but they are certainly adequate, making this a good candidate for an overnight run. Side hike potential is good in the remote desert. Running the Gila Box is a great way to

Paddle rafting in the Gila Box

start off the river running season.

Logistics: The take-out is located below the confluence of Bonita Creek and the Gila. From Solomon, AZ, just east of Safford on Highway 191/70, head north on Sanchez Road. Paved Sanchez Road bears right after crossing the river, and continues upstream. In about 7.5 miles there is a sign for the Gila Box. Stay left here on the dirt road toward Bonita Creek. It is about 2.5 miles farther to the BLM Gila Box boundary, and shortly thereafter, riverside take-out options.

To put-in on the Gila, take Highway 191 from Safford toward Clifton crossing to the north side of the river. Turn left at milepost 160 onto the Black Hills Backcountry Byway, also known as Old Safford Road. It is 4 miles from here to the river. The Old Safford Road turn is about 2.5 miles south of Clifton.

To put-in on the San Francisco, go to Clifton and launch where the river goes under the road.

Eagle Creek

Eagle Creek is a long drainage flowing due south from Arizona's southwestern reaches of the Mogollon Rim. There is a gage on the creek which indicates how rarely this stream actually runs. When the storm track locks in from the southwest, however, drainages like Eagle Creek, the Blue River, and the Gila can run high for extended periods.

The only descents I am aware of regarding Eagle Creek were made in 1992 by Wayne Van Vorhees, Glenn Rink, and Bryan Brown. They report a nice 4-day wilderness run with scenic wild surroundings, a handful of class IV rapids, and lots of class III. There is also a lower put-in that allows for a long one-day run into the Arizona Gila Box.

The upper put-in is off Upper Eagle Creek Road which leaves Highway 191 about 20 miles north of Morenci. The lower access point is off Lower Eagle Creek Road, which becomes Black River Road. This road leaves Highway 191 in Morenci.

Whitewater Rivers 231

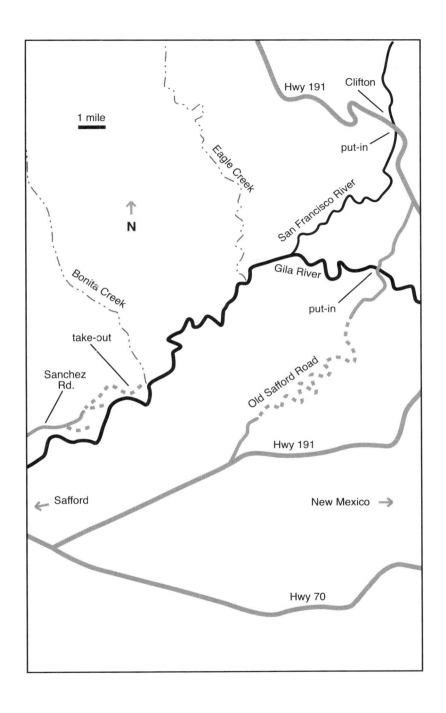

Burro Creek

General Description: A desert whitewater run in a beautiful canyon
Difficulty: III — IV
Gradient: 29 fpm / steepest mile (mile 9) is 50 fpm.
Length: 13 miles
Flow: minimum: 300 cfs
ideal: 1,000 — 2,000 cfs
Gage: Burro Creek at old Highway 93 bridge
Shuttle: Fifteen miles if using Signal Road. Seven miles of this is on a good dirt road, the rest is on pavement. A 17-Mile Road take-out makes for a twenty-one mile shuttle, four miles on pavement, and seventeen miles on dirt.
Elevation: 1,900'—1,500'
Likely Season: February, March
Peak Flow: 68,700 cfs February 9, 1993.

Burro Creek drains a large portion of western Arizona. It starts in pine-clad mountains northwest of Prescott, and runs to the low desert environs found along the section described here. For much of its course, Burro Creek cuts spectacular canyons, one of which is just downstream of the old Highway 93 bridge, the put-in for this run.

The river meanders through open desert for the first couple of miles below the put-in. There are two distinct rapids in this first section, the second of which holds good surf waves at certain levels.

At about two miles, Burro Creek enters a dramatic canyon of volcanic tuff and basalt. Beneath the sheltering canyon walls, the desert erupts in green, and blue herons can often be seen swooping over giant saguaros. The cream-colored tuff has eroded into a series of grotesque pockets emulating a giant wall of Swiss cheese, or perhaps a face of melting rock, depending on one's state of mind.

The rapids in here come after short pools. Most of the drops are class III, although at higher water levels there are two boulder-choked rapids that grow into class IV's.

About six miles into the run, Kaiser Spring Canyon (called Warm Spring Canyon on some maps) enters on the right where the river makes a sharp left turn into a significant rapid. A short hike up this side canyon will reward paddlers with a pleasant hot spring pool if it hasn't been silted in by recent floods. In case of emergency, the highway is located two miles up this side canyon.

The river canyon relents somewhat below Kaiser Spring Canyon, but the whitewater continues. A long class III (IV at higher levels) rapid starts things off before a couple miles of mellower water. Just when the day seems to be winding down, the two toughest rapids of the run appear as granite bedrock encroaches on the riverbed.

Whitewater Rivers 233

Punching into Quasar

The first class IV is a steep left to right boulder bar called Force Ten. A stout hole at the bottom makes this drop a class IV even at low water. The next rapid, however, requires higher water to come alive. Quasar is a constricted hole pinched in the granite, with creek lines available in the river right channels at higher levels.

There are still a few miles of meandering beneath rocky bluffs before Burro Creek finally breaks out into the open desert. The last couple miles could hide bothersome sandbars at low water. When the Big Sandy River enters on the right, you are less than 0.5 miles from the Signal Road take-out.

Logistics: The put-in for Burro Creek is the Burro Creek Campground on river left, next to the old Highway 93 bridge. Camping here requires a fee, but day use is free as of this writing. The turn off of Highway 93 for this campground is located a few hundred yards southeast of the new Highway 93 bridge.

The take-out is located 7 miles down Signal Road. Signal Road is well signed. It is located 8 miles south of Wikieup. When Burro Creek is running following big storms, Signal Road is often washed out where it crosses the Big Sandy River. This is 2.2 miles from Burro Creek. If the road is washed out, you must park here, and hike to the vehicles upon taking out. Hiking up the road is straightforward. Hiking up the Big Sandy is a little shorter, and generally pretty easy except for occasional quicksand. Half of the times I've run Burro Creek, I've had to do the take-out walk.

There is another take-out on river left where 17-Mile Road hits the river. I haven't used this take-out, but reports are that it is a good alternative to a washed-out Signal Road.

Whitewater Rivers 235

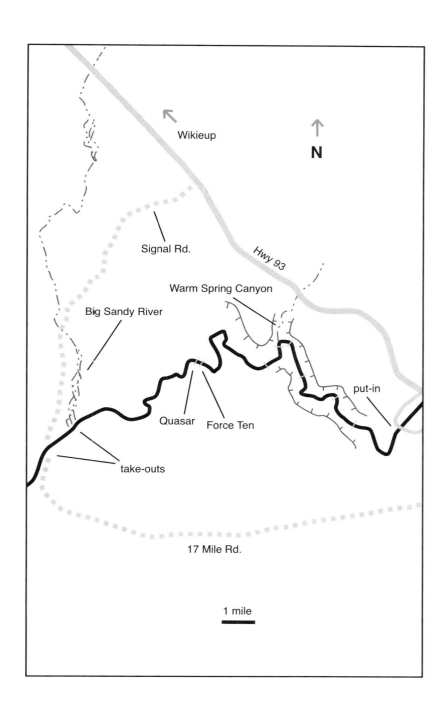

Virgin River
(Freeway Gorge)

The Virgin is a quintessential Southwestern river. It's origins are on a high spruce-covered plateau. Its tributary forks cut dramatic canyons through sandstone. Once united into a single small stream at the foot of the mountains, it is quickly diverted, sucked, and pumped to serve man's utilitarian desires. What is left of the small river then races down through desert canyons to the sun-baked flatlands before finally being swallowed by a great dead reservoir.

When the Virgin is flush with runoff, it contains some fantastic whitewater. The last of the Virgin's whitewater sections is located in the far northwestern corner of Arizona as the river cuts between the Beaver Dam and Virgin Mountains. This is a beautiful desert canyon of dark limestone cliffs, red sandstone buttes, and slopes of Joshua trees. The freeway also curves through this cut in the mountains, sharing close company with the river through most of the canyon. At the upper end of the river canyon near St. George, UT, the freeway is absent, but so is the whitewater. This upper part of the river is a nice class II float with a fish dam portage en route.

The whitewater starts at the I-15 bridge between mileposts 22 and 23. From here to Cedar Pockets, the river is often away from the freeway. The busy road is only an occasional distraction. The rapids are class II and III, mostly formed by boulder gardens. At medium to high water levels, there are sand waves that magically appear throughout the run. There is one nice limestone narrows along this stretch that definitely qualifies as a scenic highlight. Named rapids include Keyhole, Table Top, and Tree Rapid.

Look for the take-out beach just below a surfable ledge on a sharp left turn. There is a short steep trail from here up to the parking area at the Virgin River Recreation Area, otherwise known as Cedar Pockets.

The lower run starts here at Cedar Pockets. The river is mellow before things pick up as the gorge tightens. Overall, the lower run is considered a half class more difficult than the upper. A standout rapid, Big Ten (class IV at some levels), is located on a left turn just after going under a freeway bridge. Immediately below here are a series of rapids known as the Back Nine, then the river weaves directly under the freeway in the tight canyon. At the mouth of the gorge comes another significant drop called Let's Make a Deal. This is a boulder sieve rapid with a giant undercut on the left, and some logs wedged here and there. It's not as bad as it sounds though. Door number one is usually a go, but a scout is in order. The canyon opens below here, and Whorehouse Rapid leads into the basin and range desert.

Several miles remain between the end of the canyon and any reasonable take-out options. There are still a couple rapids down here, and sometimes good surf waves.

A minimum flow for the run is about 400 cfs, and the ideal range goes from 800 cfs to 1,500 cfs. The record flow is over 33,000 cfs. The Virgin usually runs in April and May, with occasional spikes following summer thunderstorms.

There is a take-out trail near private property just downstream of the freeway bridge at Littlefield, AZ. The put-in for the lower run, and take-out for the upper run, is at Cedar Pockets—exit #18. There is a $2 day-use fee here. The put-in for the upper run is just downstream from the freeway bridge between mp 22 and 23. There is enough space for three carefully parked vehicles here off the northbound lanes, just beyond the guardrail from screamin' semi-trucks!

The lowest of the Virgin River's many whitewater runs is in Arizona.

Santa Maria River
(Highway 93 run)

General Description: A relatively short run with quality rapids in the Sonoran desert
Difficulty: IV (V)
Gradient: 55 fpm/steepest gradient 100 fpm
Length: 6 miles
Flow: minimum: 300 cfs
         ideal: 600 — 800 cfs
Gage: Santa Maria near Bagdad. This gage is 10 miles downstream from the take-out.
Shuttle: 8 miles, dirt road, bikeable
Elevation: 2,100'—1,800'
Likely Season: February, March. The Santa Maria drops slower than other Arizona rivers once the basin is saturated.
Peak Flow: 23,100 cfs March 1, 1978

The Santa Maria is a logistically easy, scenic desert run with good whitewater. The granite boulder rapids are fun at low water, and continue to be runnable even at higher flows as sneak lines open up. I've run it as high as 1,700 cfs, and it was still a class IV run, with two class V's.

The rapids don't begin right away, and a little sandbar dodging is necessary to reach the gorge. When granite bluffs signal the start of the canyon, the whitewater picks up immediately. A few class II and III rapids serve as warm up for Entrance Rapid. This double ledge carries a distinctly Arizonan hazard—a cottonwood tree obstructing the right channel. Immediately below is a narrow sluice that gets nasty at medium-high flows when the hole has punch, but sneak lines haven't yet opened.

The river mellows for a bit before building back into a couple congested drops. Nicely spaced class III dominates the next mile until the river turns into an imposing gorge. Just when it appears things might get serious, they do. Two standout IV+ rapids come in quick succession, and at high water they blend into one long class V-.

The pools get longer below here, but the good drops keep coming. The bouncy around-the-corner rapid with a launchpad at the bottom was dubbed "T-Slalom" after an old Prijon was retired here after losing its stern to the bottom rock.

The last rapid—Little Buddy—is an easy V at most levels. Try not to ruin your day at this point, because only a flat mile and a half float remains to the highway bridge.

Logistics: The take-out is at the Highway 93 bridge, on river left. The put-in is about 8 to 10 miles up the dirt road that leads upstream. At the fork 0.5 miles from the take-out, bear right.

Whitewater Rivers 239

Saguaro cactus, granite, and whitewater—only in Arizona

Put-in access is a bit of a mess, because private land, catclaw, and fences separate the main road from the river. Wherever you decide to put-in, try to not anger the ranchers that live nearby. If you should encounter a local, be polite and ask permission to gain access to the river. Make sure you explain that you will be launching your boat and you will then be gone. Don't drive across their fields, and close gates behind you.

I've put in a couple different places. One spot is 2 miles beyond where the road turns north into the valley above the gorge. Turn left on a secondary dirt road 1.5 miles past the Little Maria Ranch, and you can drive another few hundred yards to park. From here it is a short carry to the water. Another put-in is reached by driving down a wash that runs just to the south of the first ranch you encounter in the south end of the valley. Bear left at the cattleguard 6 miles from the take-out, then bear left again into a wash 0.6 miles from the cattleguard. This put-in launches you closer to the canyon, but makes the hike to the water longer.

Santa Maria
(lower reaches)

Below Highway 93, the Santa Maria flows through wild desert country with a few small rapids. There are some tree islands that require quick decisions, and a couple class II+ to III- gravel bar rapids. As the river leaves the Arrastra Mountains for the open desert above Alamo Lake, shallow sand bars become the primary concern.

Stay away from this run at low water. The only time I've run it, we had about 700 cfs. One thousand cfs or more would've been better, and less than 500 cfs would've forced us to walk the last mile.

The shuttle is long, following Alamo and Sawyer Roads across endless Mojave/Sonoran Desert before reaching the river. A road leads to the water about a mile below the last of the granite bluffs, where the gage is located. Make sure you remember the take-out location. This is a remote area. Given the lengthy shuttle and mellow whitewater, this run is probably best as a two-day camping trip if there is adequate water.

Whitewater Rivers 241

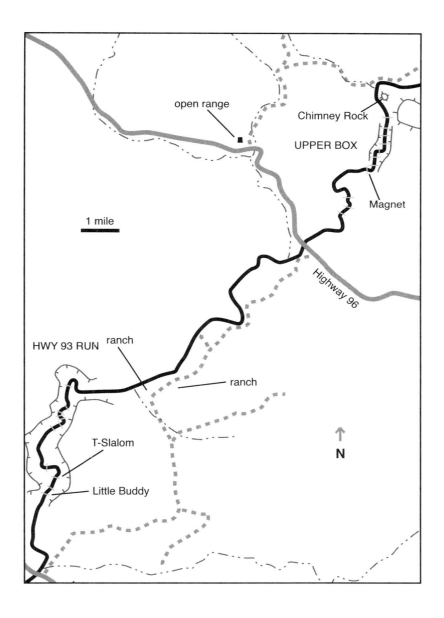

Santa Maria River
(upper box)

General Description: California granite with saguaros
Difficulty: IV — IV+ (V)
Gradient: 47fpm/steepest gradient 100 fpm
Length: 6 miles
Flow: minimum: 300 cfs
    ideal: 600 — 900 cfs
Gage: Santa Maria near Bagdad. This gage is nearly 30 miles below the take-out. To figure flows for this run, subtract about 15 percent from the gage reading. Also remember that it takes the water from this upper section several hours to reach the gage.
Shuttle: 8.6 miles, four wheel drive mandatory
Elevation: 2,500'—2,300'
Likely Season: February, March
Peak Flow: Santa Maria near Bagdad gage—23,100 cfs March 1, 1978

Lisa Gelczis, Glenn Rink, and I made a trip to western Arizona to explore some relatively unknown rivers in February of 1998. After finding quality runs on Burro Creek and the Highway 93 run on the Santa Maria, we figured this upper section of the Santa Maria was worth checking out too.

We left the pavement near the lonely ranching hamlet of Hillside, AZ, and drove down a dirt road toward a place on the map called the Muleshoe Ranch. Dozens of miles into our back road romp, we crested a rim and saw the ranch appear below us like Shangri-La. Palm trees lined the road, bright green fields covered the valley floor, and real honest-to-God cowboys acknowledged us from their saddles as we slowly approached.

The head cowboy was a friendly fellow named Stephan. We told him about the other runs we had just done, and explained to him with an air of self-satisfaction that this was to be the last in our "triple crown" of first descents. That was when he told us what he knew about the canyon. "I reckon it'll be a little tough down around Chimney Rock," he continued, "a couple boys from the ranch went down the crik in inner tubes one time, and they said it was kinda interestin' down in there." It seemed our first descent glory had been usurped before we had even put in. Slightly humbled by his story, we asked permission to launch from his property, and headed downstream in our specialized whitewater boats determined to survive the cowboy's river.

The put-in used today (pioneered by Jim McComb) avoids the long drive to the ranch, and deposits paddlers at Chimney Rock, directly above the start of the whitewater.

An impressive granite gorge closes in on the river almost immediately, and smooth boulders litter the riverbed. A couple class III rapids lead into

Whitewater Rivers 243

A trio of boaters enjoy sunshine and whitewater on the Santa Maria

the first class IV, and then the pool-drop action is constant for the next couple of miles downstream.

One of the standout drops starts with a 4-foot boof that leads into a river-wide mess of boulders. The next quarter-mile is the steepest part of the run, and can quickly turn into class V at higher flows. This steep section ends with a rapid called 7-Foot West. The boof is reminiscent of 7-Foot Falls on Georgia's Chattooga River. Unlike the Chattooga's 7-Foot, however, the boof here leads left in order to avoid a rock at the base on the right.

Below 7-Foot West is a big pool as the river exits the gorge and turns to the right. Another standout rapid lies below the pool. This one is called Magnet, as a large boulder in the runout seems to attract plastic boats.

The Santa Maria curves through the open desert for a mile or more before entering the granite again. There is some good class III in this final gorge, then a mile of flatwater to the take-out at Highway 96.

Logistics: The take-out is the Highway 96 bridge over the Santa Maria. To reach the put-in, drive northwest up the highway for 3.1 miles and turn right onto a dirt road with an "open range" oven nearby. Bear right at any forks in the road, and you will arrive at the Santa Maria 5.5 miles from the highway.

Once leaving the pavement, the road steadily climbs up a small drainage before bending south and following Sycamore Wash down to the river. There are a couple creek crossings on Sycamore Wash that can be difficult except for good four wheel drives with good drivers.

See map on page 241.

Bill Williams River

The Bill Williams River emerges from beneath Alamo Reservoir and flows west to the Colorado River at Lake Havasu. Normally there is only 25 cfs released from the dam at Alamo, but when excessive inflows raise the lake level, the dam operators give life back to the river.

Below the dam, the river runs through a neat canyon of hard metamorphic rock. Low stream gradient keeps the whitewater mellow (surging class II) in here, although higher flows might produce some interesting hydraulics. At the 3,000 cfs we had, it was a swift float to the mouth of the canyon. You could probably take out in Reid Valley downstream of the canyon, but I haven't investigated it. We floated almost all the way to the Colorado River at Lake Havasu.

Riparian growth clutters the riverbed for the next several miles below Reid Valley. With attentive paddling, I was able to stay in my boat at all but one tree sieve where I had to drag over the sand to a clear channel.

A couple miles below a big pipeline that crosses over the river, the trees lessen. For the next several miles, the Bill Williams resembles a typical Western river—wide and open with beautiful big desert scenery.

Once past Black Mesa, the water gets spread thin as it meanders across a broad sandy wash. The more water the better in here. At 2,000 cfs, you will probably be forced to drag a couple times in these six wide sandy miles.

If you had enough water for the sand flats, you'll probably have too much for the canyon below. As the river cuts through the Bill Williams Mountains, it gets swift and treacherous as it careens through a riparian forest. Although there are few true rapids, significant paddling skill is required to weave around the rapidly approaching strainers.

The stream slows and opens somewhat as it begins to meander in its last few miles, and then the jungle closes in for good. We lost the channel (we aren't sure one exists) a couple miles short of Lake Havasu. We stayed left as the water continued to sieve through impenetrable thickets of tamarisk and willow to our right. Finally our channel ended, and we were left stranded amidst the flooded riparian forest.

After a 20-minute hack with loaded kayaks through the swamp, we gave up finding a boatable channel, and retreated to the desert on river left, where we found the Bill Williams River Road. From here we walked 3 miles out to the highway and our waiting shuttle driver.

If you decide to run the entire Bill Williams, be sure and check the downstream gage (Bill Williams near Parker) to see if the water is making it that far. For the first few days of release, the river sinks into the sand once past the initial canyon.

Grand Canyon

What can one say about Grand Canyon? The place is awesome, mind-blowing, surreal. Even those superlatives don't do it justice. If you haven't been there, you should go.

The biggest obstacle to floating through Grand Canyon is obtaining a permit. Enter the lottery at www.nps.gov/grca/planyourvisit/weightedlottery.htm to take your chance at a permit. If you can't get your own permit, you can always go with an outfitter. If you can't afford an outfitter, you can always just go hiking.

If you do get a permit to run the river, there are a variety of sources to consult relating to the river and canyon. My contribution to the morass is *Grand Canyon River Hikes*. Check it out for all the great side hikes available down there.

Besides the main river, there are several paddleable side streams within Grand Canyon. The Little Colorado is the most obvious run. Consult details in this book.

Bright Angel Creek flows high enough to float in springtime during good years, but it doesn't look that interesting, and the rangers probably wouldn't like you causing a disturbance in the busy Phantom Ranch corridor either.

Shinumo Creek cranks in the spring too. You'd have to hike your shuttle, and it has plenty of brush. The one interesting drop comes right at the end, where the creek enters a narrows and plunges over a 10-footer that sometimes collects logs—not real appealing.

Tapeats Creek has been run several times, and its gorge is spectacular. If you're feeling wacky and want to carry boats up to the top of the gorge, here's my advice: Although it has been run at higher water, it is probably best done at base flow (60cfs?) in inflatable kayaks. During spring runoff, it quickly becomes too high. I once hauled a borrowed boat to the head of the canyon and turned back, because it looked too gnarly. On the way back down the trail, a gust of wind grabbed my unattended boat and blew it off the edge into the gorge. Fortunately a kayaker from another trip corralled the boat as it hit the Colorado, and we recovered all the gear. A 200-footer into three feet of water leaves a mark though. My Tapeats Creek attempt turned out to be nothing more than an expensive hike with a kayak.

Kanab Creek would be a spectacular multi-day run, but it rarely has enough water.

Havasu Creek's base flow is 70 cfs, not quite enough for the travertine riverbed. I once ran the last half-mile on 120 cfs following rains, and it was a blast. One might be able to catch it at higher water during a wet winter, but put-in logistics are always difficult.

Of course, to legally float any of these side streams into the Colorado, you need a permit once you hit the Colorado, making logistics next to impossible. Like I said, Grand Canyon is a good place for hiking.

Whitewater Rivers 247

Alive below Lava

Other Titles From Funhog Press

Funhog Press is a small, independently owned publisher based in Flagstaff, Arizona. We are dedicated to the production of quality guides with an original voice. Thank you for your support.

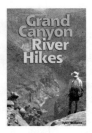

This is the book for finding just the right side hikes on your Grand Canyon river trip. As with all Funhog Press books, maps and photos accompany every route description.

Both easy streamside trails and technical gorges are covered in this complete guidebook.

Whitewater Classics is part guide book, part story book, and part history book, featuring whitewater destinations from Mexico to Alaska. Color photos and maps accompany the text for all fifty classic rivers.

A guide to the mountains, peaks and high points of Southern Arizona.

To order Funhog books:
- visit www.funhogpress.com
- ask for them at your local bookstore
- ask for them at your local outfitter
- use this order form

Arizona Summits:South $19.95 _____
Canyoneering Arizona $19.95 _____
Grand Canyon River Hikes $18.95 _____
Whitewater Classics $26.95 _____
Sub total _____
AZ residents add 8.3% tax _____
Shipping $3 for 1 book, $1 for each additional _____

Send check or money order to Funhog Press, 2819 N. Center St., Flagstaff, AZ 86004